SCIENTIFIC AMERICAN EXPLORES BIG IDEAS

The Science of Death

Published in 2025 by Scientific American Educational Publishing
in association with **The Rosen Publishing Group**
2544 Clinton Street, Buffalo NY 14224

Contains material from Scientific American®, a division of Springer Nature America, Inc., reprinted by permission, as well as original material from The Rosen Publishing Group®.

First Edition

Scientific American
Lisa Pallatroni: Project Editor

Rosen Publishing
Erica Grove: Compiling Editor
Michael Moy: Senior Graphic Designer

Cataloging-in-Publication Data

Names: Scientific American, Inc.
Title: The science of death / edited by the Scientific American Editors.
Description: First edition. | New York : Scientific American Educational Publishing, 2025. | Series: Scientific American explores big ideas | Includes glossary and index.
Identifiers: ISBN 9781538312896 (pbk.) | ISBN 9781538312902 (library bound)| ISBN 9781538312919 (ebook)
Subjects: LCSH: Death–Juvenile literature. | Death–Psychological aspects–Juvenile literature.
Classification: LCCBF723.D3 S354 2025 | DDC 155.9'37–dc23

Manufactured in the United States of America
Websites listed were live at the time of publication.

Cover: peterschreiber.media/Shutterstock.com and natrot/iStock.com

CPSIA Compliance Information: Batch # CW25SA.
For Further Information contact Rosen Publishing at 1-800-237-9932.

CONTENTS

INTRODUCTION

Death has long been a source of intrigue and fear. It is the driving force for everything from horror movies to religions. It is both inevitable and unknowable—it is impossible for any living being to conceptualize what it feels like to experience death or what they will experience in its aftermath with any scientific certainty. Unfortunately, not even science can prevent it from happening, tell us what it's like to die, or explain what happens to the soul after death. But it can make certain aspects of death less mysterious—including questions around what happens to the body and mind during death—and it can play an essential role in ensuring that more people get the opportunity to live long and satisfying lives. This volume offers information from experts showing advancements in our understanding of these aspects of death.

Section 1, "Death and the Body," looks at what physically happens to someone when they are dying and after they have died. Section 2, "Death and the Mind," takes a similar approach to the topic but examines the role of the brain in death and dying. The next two sections zoom out on the topic. Section 3, "Mass Death," considers some of the events and variables that have led to large groups of people dying, in some cases unnecessarily, or that could lead to many deaths. Section 4, "Preventing Death," considers potential societal and lifestyle changes that can help people live longer, healthier lives and avoid unnecessary deaths. Finally, Section 5, "Cheating Death and Life After Death," examines situations in which people have narrowly and unexpectedly avoided death, attempts to use science to considerably prolong life, and scientific approaches to questions about the afterlife.

The awareness of mortality is one of the greatest and most widespread existential crises that occur. Its mysterious and inevitable nature makes it a source of fear but also a source of meaning for life. This volume attempts to make the topic slightly less mysterious by offering scientific answers to a few of the many questions we have about death.

Section 1: Death and the Body

Dust to Dust: The Brief, Eventful Afterlife of a Human Corpse

By Arpad A. Vass

Welcome or not, dying is a natural part of the circle of life. Death initiates a complex process by which the human body gradually reverts back to dust, as it were. In the language of forensics, decomposition transforms our biological structures into simple organic and inorganic building blocks that plants and animals can use.

Four main factors affect the pace and completeness of decay. The most important is temperature: the rate of chemical reactions in a cadaver doubles with each 10 degree Celsius rise. Humidity or water from the environment buffers those reactions, slowing their effects. Extreme acidity or alkalinity hastens how quickly enzymes degrade biological molecules–although again, the presence of ample water can mediate the effects. Finally, anything that blocks exposure to oxygen, such as burial, submersion, or high altitude, will slow decomposition. Depending on the interplay of these four factors, the body can turn into a skeleton as rapidly as two weeks or take more than two years.

Forensic scientists use their knowledge of the biology and chemistry of decomposition, together with the variables that affect the speed of decay, to estimate a person's time of death and to help investigators discover clandestine graves. Medical experts and ethicists may not agree on how to define the moment of death, but they know in great detail the stages through which a body gradually decomposes. The stages are described below. The timescales noted are approximate and refer to a body that is lying open to the air. Being buried unshrouded in soil or in a casket could extend the intervals significantly.

Stage 1: Fresh—Days 1 to 6

In the first stage, soft tissue begins to decompose in a chain of events that starts with autolysis, or self-digestion. When breathing and circulation cease, cells are left without a supply of oxygen. The cells survive for a few minutes to a few days, but they can no longer pass wastes into the bloodstream. Carbon dioxide, one of the by-products of metabolism, is acidic, and as it accumulates, the acidity inside a cell increases, causing cell membranes to rupture. Single membranes surrounding organelles called lysosomes tend to dissolve first. The sacs contain digestive enzymes normally used by cells to break down organic molecules such as proteins. As these enzymes spill out, they begin digesting the cell from the inside out, eventually creating small blisters in and on internal tissues and organs and on the skin. The blister fluid, consisting of digested cell innards, is rich in nutrients.

As blisters rupture, the fluids give the surface of the corpse a moisture-laden sheen. Deep skin cells begin to slough off, resulting in skin slippage, one of the first visually revolting signs of decomposition.

Within a few hours after death, several other phenomena also begin. Muscles stiffen (rigor mortis), starting in the eyelids, jaw, and neck, when cells no longer pump out calcium ions; such pumping keeps muscles supple. For a time, muscle cells continue to convert nutrients into energy, but without oxygen the process produces lactic acid, which also causes muscles to contract. Gelling of the cell's innards, resulting from increased acidity, contributes to the stiffening. Rigor mortis peaks in 24 hours but then relaxes as cells succumb to autolysis.

The body also starts to cool (algor mortis) to ambient temperature, generally at approximately 0.8 degree C per hour. Algor mortis can of course be influenced by the body's location and size, clothing and weather conditions.

Within an hour or two of death, the pull of gravity makes red and white blood cells settle (livor mortis), gradually giving a purplish-red hue to the epidermis, except in areas that are being compressed, such as skin in contact with the ground. Maximum congealing takes place at six to 12 hours. Marbling occurs after several days as blood and proteins begin to decompose and liberate sulfur-rich compounds, giving the corpse one of its offensive odors.

Stage 2: Bloat—Days 7 to 23

After about a week, the release of those nutrient-rich fluids begins to fuel an army of microbes that further liquefy the body's soft tissue. Bacteria, fungi, and protozoa (from the corpse and from the environment) attack the tissue, producing numerous gases, including carbon dioxide, methane, hydrogen sulfide, ammonia, and a variety of so-called volatile organic compounds such as benzene. Because the greatest concentration of microbes in the body is in the intestinal tract, the most obvious bloating, or distension, occurs there. Trapped gases can eventually erupt from the rectum or even rip apart the abdominal wall.

Stage 3: Active Decay—Days 24 to 50

During this stage, insects (primarily maggots and beetles) and sometimes carnivores join microorganisms in removing the remaining traces of tissue. Much of the body's muscle and fat has been reduced to a foul-smelling, liquidy pastelike substance. If the tissue has been open to air (aerobic conditions), it will have a pH greater than 9.0, highly basic (7.0 is neutral). If the corpse has been buried so that anaerobic (oxygen-free) conditions prevail, the body will be acidic (less than 7.0). The more extreme the pH, the quicker the decomposition.

If conditions are basic and also warm and moist, lipids (primarily triglycerides) will go through a chemical reaction called saponification that creates adipocere, also known as grave wax. (The reaction is the basis for how commercial soap is made from animal fat.) Adipocere can range in color from whitish to dark yellow, with the occasional brown chunk here and there. It can also have a variety of consistencies, from hard and crumbly if decomposition has progressed rapidly to soft and pasty for slower decay. If grave wax covers decomposing tissue, it will create an anaerobic environment and shield the tissue from its surroundings, retarding the process and potentially delaying complete liquefaction at that site for years.

Stage 4: Dry—Days 51 to 64

In the dry stage, the last traces of tissue are removed, leaving the human skeleton. Odors and disfigurement are largely gone. Bones then go through their own decomposition process, called diagenesis, which can last years to decades. Bone has two components: protein (collagen) and a mineral, hydroxyapatite. Protein degrades first, which leaves the remaining skeletal material susceptible to cracking and flaking. Once the protein is gone, freezing and thawing, moisture, carnivores, and erosion will break it down into dust. But if the bones lie in soil that is very dry and contains certain minerals, the minerals can fill in the cracks and voids, bonding the hydroxyapatite and allowing the combination to fossilize and survive the ravages of time.

Time of Death?

Forensic scientists like myself study decomposing bodies to improve our methods for accurately determining how long someone has been dead and for finding clandestine graves. We have identified more than 400 chemicals released during decomposition that give us clues for both tasks. My laboratory has also created an electronic handheld instrument (called Labrador) that can detect many of these compounds. About 30 of the chemicals, when identified together, provide very good evidence that hidden human remains have been found. Among them:

- **Freons.** These molecules are similar to the coolant in your refrigerator or air conditioner and accumulate (in inert form) in tissue and bone matrixes during a lifetime of ingesting fluoridated water or products such as toothpaste.

- **Aromatic Hydrocarbons.** Human decomposition has a unique, sickly sweet odor, largely created by aromatics such as benzene, an important component of gasoline.
- **Sulfur compounds.** The same dimethyl disulfides and hydrogen sulfides released by decaying vegetation in swamps and bogs contribute a rotten-egg smell.
- **Carbon Tetrachloride.** Created by bacteria during decomposition, this nasty compound was once used in fire extinguishers, as a dry-cleaning solvent, and in making chlorofluorocarbons (which partially destroyed the ozone layer). It is now banned from most applications because it is highly toxic and can even cause cancer. How ironic that after a lifetime of health-conscious living, we revert to this and other known carcinogens.

"Necrobiome" Reveals a Corpse's Time of Death

By Christopher Intagliata

Tens of trillions of microbes call our living bodies home. But when we die? "The first thing that happens is basically ecosystem collapse—where you have a tremendous loss of diversity." Nathan Lents, a molecular biologist at John Jay College in New York. "And then it bottoms out and starts to get rich again."

That microbial phoenix, rising from our extinguished mortal coils, is called the "necrobiome." Lents and his team tracked the necrobiome, by swabbing the ears and noses of 21 cadavers at a body farm in Tennessee. It's a sort of outdoor lab for forensic scientists, where bodies are left to the elements to decompose.

They tracked the genetic signatures of that microbial community as it waned and waxed after death. And they used that data to build an algorithm that could pinpoint a corpse's time of death, to an accuracy of just two summertime days. "And that held out for up to six to seven weeks. And that's way better than entomology can tell you." Entomology being the study of the insects that colonize a corpse. "Entomology's okay for giving you upper and lower limits within five to seven days, but beyond that, entomology's not helpful."

The study is in the journal *PLoS ONE*. [Hunter R. Johnson et al., A Machine Learning Approach for Using the Postmortem Skin Microbiome to Estimate the Postmortem Interval]

The method isn't quite ready for primetime. There's still a lot of 'biological noise' in the system. "We're talking about living things here. Well ... living and dead things." But as with any machine learning, more info will help it see beyond the noise. "It will forever learn. So the more data we pump into this system, the better it will get." Ultimately, Lents says, the algorithm will have to be smart enough to hold up in a court of law, when it could determine the fate of someone accused of turning someone into a corpse.

[The above text is a transcript of the podcast Science Quickly.]

Why Humans Live So Long

By Heather Pringle

On a Sunday morning in a decaying and dangerous inner-city barrio in Lima, Peru, an unmarked white van carrying nearly a dozen bodies rumbles to a stop on the grounds of the National Institute of Neurological Sciences. Seated in a small waiting area to the rear of the building, a throng of well-dressed researchers and government officials watches intently. As the driver clambers out, an assistant hustles off in search of a hospital gurney. Within minutes, two men wheel the first body into the institute's imaging unit.

Onlooker Caleb Finch, a biologist at the University of Southern California, has been waiting for this moment for months. Tall, gaunt, and graying, with a Father Time–style beard, the 75-year-old scientist has devoted his career to the study of human aging. Our kind is remarkably long-lived compared with other primates. Our nearest surviving relatives, the chimpanzees, have a life expectancy at birth of about 13 years. In contrast, babies born in the U.S. in 2009 possessed a life expectancy at birth of 78.5 years. Finch has come to Lima to find out why–by peering into the distant past. The cadavers in the van belong to men, women, and children who perished along this stretch of coastal desert as much as 1,800 years ago, long before the Spanish conquest. Cocooned in dusty textiles and interred in arid desert tombs, their naturally mummified bodies preserve critical new clues to the mystery of human longevity. As envoys from an era long before modern health care, they will offer case studies of aging in the past. Finch walks over to the van, grinning as he surveys the cargo. "That's a pack of mummies," he says.

Most researchers chalk up our supersized lifespan to the advent of vaccines, antibiotics, and other medical advances, the development of efficient urban sanitation systems, and the availability of fresh, nutritious vegetables and fruit year-round. Indeed, much demographic evidence shows that these factors greatly extended human life over the past 200 years. But critical as they were to extending human life, they are only part of the longevity puzzle, Finch warrants. Marshaling data from fields as diverse as physical anthropology, primatology, genetics, and medicine, he now proposes a controversial new hypothesis: that the trend toward slower aging and longer lives began much, much earlier, as our human ancestors evolved an increasingly powerful defense system to fight off the many pathogens and irritants in ancient environments. If Finch is right, future research on the complex links among infection, host defense, and the chronic diseases of the elderly may revolutionize scientists' understanding of aging and how to cope with the challenges it brings.

And Many More

Hints that modern health practices might not be solely responsible for our long lifespan have come from studies of contemporary hunter-gatherer groups. In 1985 Nicholas Blurton-Jones, a biological anthropologist at the University of California, Los Angeles, set off by Land Rover across the trackless bush in Tanzania's Lake Eyasi basin. With field assistant Gudo Mahiya, Blurton-Jones traveled to the isolated camps of the Hadza, hunter-gatherers who lived much as their ancestors had, hunting baboons and wildebeest, digging starchy tubers and collecting honey during the rainy season from hives of the African honeybee. Journeying from one camp to another, the two researchers collected basic demographic data, checking each Hadza household and recording the names and ages of the inhabitants. Then the pair updated this census information six times in the 15 years that followed, noting down the names of all who had died and the causes of their death. In addition, Blurton-Jones obtained some earlier census data on the Hadza from two other researchers.

The Hadza lived–as ancient humans and chimpanzees did–in a natural environment teeming with pathogens and parasites. They lacked running water and sewage systems, defecating in a zone 20 to 40 meters away from their camps, and they rarely sought out medical care. Yet as Blurton-Jones and Mahiya discovered, the Hadza enjoyed much longer lives than chimpanzees did. Indeed, the Hadza had a life expectancy at birth of 32.7 years. And if they reached adulthood, they could expect to live 40 more years, nearly three times longer than a chimpanzee reaching adulthood. Some Hadza elders survived into their 80s. Clearly, their relatively long lives owed little to medical and technological advances.

Moreover, the Hadza were not alone. In 2007 two anthropologists, Michael Gurven of U.C. Santa Barbara and Hillard Kaplan of the University of New Mexico analyzed data from all five modern hunter-gatherer societies that researchers had studied demographically. Infections counted for 72 percent of the deaths, and each group revealed a very similar J-shaped mortality curve–with child mortality as high as 30 percent, low death rates in early adulthood, and exponentially rising mortality after the age of 40. Then Gurven and Kaplan compared these curves with those of both wild and captive chimpanzees: the simians experienced the sharp uptick of adult mortality at least 10 years earlier than human hunter-gatherers. "It appears that chimpanzees age much faster than humans," concluded Gurven and Kaplan in their paper detailing the findings, "and die earlier, even in protected environments."

Yet when, exactly, did humans begin living longer? To obtain clues, anthropologists Rachel Caspari of Central Michigan University and Sang-Hee Lee of U.C. Riverside examined the remains of 768 individuals from four ancestral human groups spanning millions of years. By assessing the degree of dental wear, which accumulates at a constant pace from chewing, they estimated the ratio of young adults around 15 years of age to older adults around age 30 (old enough to be a grandparent) in each of the four groups. Their studies revealed that living to 30 and beyond became common only recently in our prehistoric past. Among the australopithecines, which emerged in Africa around 4.4 million years ago, most individuals died before their 30th birthday. Moreover, the ratio of 30–somethings to 15-year-olds was just 0.12. In contrast, *Homo sapiens* who roamed

Europe between 44,000 and 10,000 years ago often lived to 30 or more, achieving a ratio of 2.08

Calculating the life expectancy of early *H. sapiens* populations is challenging, however: detailed demographic data, such as those supplied by both census records and death registrations, are lacking for much of our long past. So Finch and his colleague Eileen Crimmins, a gerontologist at the University of Southern California, analyzed the earliest, virtually complete statistical set of that nature available–data first gathered in Sweden in 1751, decades before the advent of modern medicine and hygiene. The study revealed that mid-18th-century Swedes had a life expectancy at birth of 35. But those who survived bacterial infections and contagious diseases such as smallpox during childhood and reached the age of 20 could reasonably look forward to another 40 years.

To Finch, these findings raised a major question. The 18th-century Swedes lived cheek by jowl in large, permanent villages, towns, and cities, where they were exposed to serious health risks unknown to small communities of mobile chimpanzees. So why did the Swedes live longer? The answer, it turns out, may lie in the meaty diets of their early human ancestors and the evolution of genes that protected them from the many hazards of carnivory.

Meat-Eating Genes

Chimpanzees spend most of their waking hours in a sweet pursuit: foraging for figs and other ripe fruits. In search of fructose-rich fare, they range over large territories, only occasionally using the same night nest twice in a row. They are skilled at hunting small mammals such as the red colobus monkey, but they do not deliberately set out searching for these prey. Nor do they consume large quantities of meat. Primatologists studying wild chimpanzees in Tanzania have calculated that meat makes up 5 percent or less of the simians' annual diet there, whereas research in Uganda shows that animal fat constitutes only 2.5 percent of their yearly fare by dry weight.

In all likelihood, Finch says, the earliest members of the human family consumed a similar plant-based diet. Yet sometime between 3.4 million and 2.5 million years ago, our ancestors incorporated a major new source of animal protein. As sites in Ethiopia show, they began butchering the remains of large, hoofed mammals such as antelopes with simple stone tools, smashing the bones to get at the fat-rich marrow, slicing off strips of meat, and leaving behind telltale cut marks on femurs and ribs. And by 1.8 million years ago, if not earlier, humans began actively hunting large game and bringing entire carcasses back to camp. The new abundance of calories and protein most likely helped to fuel brain growth but also increased exposure to infections. Finch suggests that this risk favored the rise and spread of adaptations that allowed our predecessors to survive attacks by pathogens and thus live longer.

The trend toward increasing carnivory would have exposed our ancestors to pathogens in several ways. Early humans who scavenged the carcasses of dead animals, and who dined on raw meat and viscera, boosted their chances of ingesting infectious pathogens. Moreover, as humans took up hunting large animals, they faced greater risks of lacerations and fractured bones when closing in on their prey: such injuries could lead to deadly infections. Even cookery, which may have emerged as early as 1 million years ago, if not earlier, posed perils. Inhaling wood smoke daily exposes humans to high levels of endotoxins and soot particles. Roasting and charring meat improves both the taste and digestibility but creates chemical modifications known as advanced glycation end products, which contribute to serious diseases such as diabetes. Our ancestors' later embrace of agriculture and animal husbandry, which began some 11,500 years ago, added new dangers. The daily proximity of humans to domesticated goats, sheep, pigs, cattle, and chickens, for example, elevated the risk of contracting bacterial and viral infections from animals. Moreover, as families settled permanently in villages, sewage from humans and livestock contaminated local water supplies. Pathogenic bacteria thrived.

Even so, humans exposed to such health risks in 1751 in Sweden lived longer than their simian relatives. To tease out clues to this longevity, Finch began studying the scientific literature on chimpanzee and human genomes. Previously published studies by others showed that the two genomes were around 99 percent identical. But in the uniquely human 1 percent, evolutionary biologist Hernán Dopazo, then at the Prince Felipe Research Center in Valencia, Spain, and his colleagues discerned a disproportionately high number of genes that had undergone positive selection and that played key roles in host defense and immunity–specifically in a part of the defense system known as the inflammatory response. Positive selection favors genes that hone our ability to survive and reproduce, which allows them to become more frequent in populations over time, a process that leaves a distinctive "signature" in the DNA sequence. Dopazo's findings added new weight to an idea growing in Finch's mind. He wondered if natural selection had endowed ancient humans with a souped-up system for fighting off the microbial threats and warding off other health hazards posed by increased meat consumption, thereby extending our lifespan.

In the war against bacteria, viruses, and other microbes that seek to invade our tissues, the human host defense system brandishes two powerful weapons: the innate immune system and the adaptive immune system. The innate system is the first responder. It mobilizes immediately at the scene of an attack or injury to eliminate pathogens and heal damaged tissue, and it essentially responds in the same way to all threats. The adaptive system, in contrast, kicks into gear more slowly, customizing its response to particular pathogens. In doing so, it creates an immunological memory that confers lifelong protection against the invader.

The inflammatory response is part of the innate immune system. It goes to work when tissues suffer damage from microbes, traumatic wounds, injuries, or toxins, and, as Finch points out, physicians have long recognized its hallmarks. Some 2,000 years ago Aulus Cornelius Celsus, a Roman medical author, described four cardinal signs of inflammation–heat, redness, swelling, and pain. The heat and redness come from a swift and marked increase in the flow of warm blood to the damaged tissue. Swelling then results from increased vascular permeability, which causes blood cells and plasma to leak into the affected area, carrying proteins that can assist in preventing the spread of infection and in initiating wound healing.

Finch began examining the human-specific changes in genes related to host defense. He was quickly struck by the changes that had affected the *apolipoprotein E (APOE)* gene. This important gene strongly influences the transport and metabolism of lipids, the development of the brain, and the workings of the immune system. It has three primary, uniquely human variants (alleles), of which *APOE* e4 and *APOE* e3 are the most prevalent.

APOE e4's DNA sequences closely resemble those in chimpanzee *APOE*, strongly suggesting that it is the ancestral human variant that emerged near the beginning of the *Homo* genus more than 2 million years ago and thus may have had the earliest effect on our longevity. Differing in several critical amino acids from the chimp version, *APOE* e4 vigorously ramps up the acute phase of inflammation. It boosts the production of proteins such as interleukin-6, which helps to increase body temperature, and tumor necrosis factor–alpha, which induces fever and inhibits viruses from replicating. Equipped with this supercharged defense system, children in ancient human families had a better chance of fighting off harmful microbes that they unwittingly ingested in food and encountered in their surroundings. "When humans left the canopy and went out onto the savanna," Finch notes, "they had a much higher exposure to infectious stimuli. The savanna is knee-deep in herbivore dung, and humans were out there in bare feet."

Moreover, early humans who carried *APOE* e4 most likely profited in another key way. This variant facilitates both the intestinal absorption of lipids and the efficient storage of fat in body tissue. During times when game was scarce and hunting poor, early *APOE* e4 carriers could draw on this banked fat, upping the odds of their survival.

Even today children who carry *APOE* e4 enjoy an advantage over those who do not. In one study of youngsters from impoverished families living in a Brazilian shantytown, *APOE* e4 carriers succumbed to fewer bouts of diarrheal disease brought on by *Escherichia coli* or *Giardia* infections than noncarriers did. And they scored higher on cognitive tests, most likely as a result of their greater absorption of cholesterol—a dietary requirement for neurons to develop in the brain. "So this would have been adaptive, we think," Finch remarks.

A Deferred Cost

All told, *APOE* e4 seems to be a key part of the puzzle of human longevity. Ironically, now that we live longer, this gene variant appears to double-cross us later in life. Its debilitating effects became apparent only as our human ancestors increasingly survived to middle age and beyond. In Lima, Finch and an international team of cardiologists, radiologists, biologists, and anthropologists are searching for traces of these afflictions in the preserved cardiovascular tissues of ancient adult mummies.

Inside the crowded imaging unit in Lima, Finch hovers over a technician's computer. It has been a long, trying morning. Several of the mummy bundles transported to the unit are too large to fit into the CT scanner. Others, when scanned, reveal little more than skeletal remains, raising doubts that the preservation of human tissue in the bundles will be adequate for the study.

But no one is giving up. On the screen is a crisp, three-dimensional CT scan of a bundle just wheeled in from the van. Hunching forward, cardiologists Gregory Thomas of Long Beach Memorial Medical Center in California and Randall C. Thompson of the University of Missouri School of Medicine–Kansas City scrutinize an anatomical landscape rendered strangely foreign by centuries of decay and desiccation. As the technician scrolls up and down the image, the two cardiologists gradually pick out preserved soft tissue and the snaking trails of major arteries. The relief in the room is palpable. Then, unable to resist, the two cardiologists take a quick preliminary look along the arteries for small, dense, white patches—calcified plaque that signals an advanced stage of atherosclerosis, or hardening of the arteries, the leading cause of fatal heart attacks and strokes. The individual has clearly calcified arteries.

Cardiologists have traditionally regarded atherosclerosis as a disease of modern civilization. Contemporary behaviors such as smoking cigarettes, eschewing exercise, dining on high-calorie diets and packing on the pounds are all known to increase the risk of this disease. Moreover, several recent studies point to an emerging atherosclerosis epidemic in the developing world, as societies there grow more affluent and increasingly embrace a modern, Western lifestyle. Yet in 2010 Thomas and a group of his colleagues decided to test the idea that atherosclerosis is a disease of modern, affluent life by taking CT scans of ancient human mummies and examining their arteries.

The team started in Egypt, with 52 mummies dating between 3,500 and 2,000 years ago. Biological anthropologist Muhammad Al-Tohamy Soliman of the National Research Center in Giza estimated the age at death for each individual, based on an examination of dental and skeletal development. Then the medical team pored over the scans. Discussing the images during weekly Skype calls, they identified cardiovascular tissue in nearly 85 percent of the mummies. To their surprise, 45 percent of these had definite or probable atherosclerosis—clear evidence that one ancient population suffered from the disease. "We were [also] a bit surprised by just how much atherosclerosis we found in ancient Egyptians who were young," recalls team member James Sutherland, a radiologist at the South Coast Radiological Medical Group in Laguna Hills, Calif. "The average age of death was around 40."

When their paper came out in the *Journal of the American College of Cardiology* in the spring of 2011, Finch contacted the team immediately, proposing a new explanation for the high levels of atherosclerosis detected in the study. The ancient Egyptians, Finch noted, were no strangers to pestilence and infection. Previous studies showed that many ancient Egyptians were exposed to a wide range of infectious diseases, including malaria, tuberculosis, and schistosomiasis (an ailment caused by tiny parasitic worms found in contaminated water). *APOE* e4 carriers, with their enhanced immune systems, tended to survive many childhood infections. But they experienced decades' worth of chronic high levels of inflammation in the pathogen-rich environment—levels that are now linked to several deadly diseases of old age, including atherosclerosis and Alzheimer's. Indeed, the arterial plaques that characterize atherosclerosis seem to accumulate during inflammation and wound healing in the vascular wall. "And while it might be pushing it to say the senile plaques of Alzheimer's are some form of scab, like the plaques on artery vessels, they have many of the same components," Finch suggests.

Thomas and his colleagues asked Finch to join their team. Together they decided to gather more data, examining the cardiovascular tissues of ancient mummies from a wide range of cultures. The Egyptians in their first study likely came from affluent upper classes that could afford mummification: such individuals may have exercised rarely and dined frequently on high-calorie foods. So the team expanded the study to other, very different cultures. They examined existing CT scans of ancestral Puebloan mummies from Utah and century-old Unangan mummies from Alaska. In addition, they analyzed the scans they had taken of pre-Hispanic mummies from coastal Peru. Those individuals dated to as early as 1500 BCE.

In March 2013 the team published its findings in the *Lancet*. Among the 137 examined mummies, 34 percent had probable or definite atherosclerosis. Significantly, the scans revealed the disease in all four ancient populations, including the hunting-and-gathering Unangan people, who ate a largely marine diet. The findings clearly challenged the idea that atherosclerosis was a modern disease and pointed to another explanation. "The high level of chronic infection and inflammation in premodern conditions might have promoted the inflammatory aspects of atherosclerosis," the team wrote.

Perhaps, Finch says, the ancient gene variant that ramped up our inflammatory response and boosted the chances of our survival to the age of reproduction–*APOE* e4–came with a steep, deferred cost: heart attacks, strokes, and other chronic diseases of aging. In fact, *APOE* e4 appears to be a classic case of something biologists call antagonistic pleiotropy, in which a gene has a strong positive effect on the young and an adverse impact on the old. "I think these are very intriguing ideas," says Steven N. Austad, a biologist and gerontologist at the University of Alabama at Birmingham. "And what evidence we have supports them."

Refining Immune Response

Research also points to other gene variants that contributed to our longevity. At roughly the same time that *H. sapiens* emerged in Africa some 200,000 years ago, a second major *APOE* variant emerged. This allele, known as *APOE* e3, enhanced health among adults in the 40- to 70-year-old range and helped to slow the aging process, and today it has a prevalence of between 60 and 90 percent in human populations. As Finch points out, *APOE* e3 carriers produce a less vigorous inflammatory response than those with the ancestral variant. Moreover, they appear better adapted to meat- and fat-rich diets. Generally speaking, they have lower blood cholesterol and are less prone to the diseases that strip the old of their vitality: coronary heart disease, cognitive decline, and Alzheimer's. Indeed, carriers of the more recent variant enjoy life expectancies as much as six years longer than their *APOE* e4 neighbors. "*APOE* e3," Finch notes, "may have been a factor in the evolution of long lifespans."

APOE is not the only gene linked to the evolution of human longevity, however. At U.C. San Diego, Ajit Varki, a professor of medicine, and his colleagues are investigating several other genes that may have undergone changes that boosted our chances of survival and extended our lives. Varki's research focuses on the *SIGLEC* genes that play key roles related to host defense. These genes express proteins that straddle our cell membranes and act a little like sentries. Their function "is to recognize friends, not foes," Varki explains. It is no easy matter. To fool these sentries, infectious pathogens evolve camouflage consisting of proteins that mimic those borne by "friends."

In 2012 Varki and his team published a study in the *Proceedings of the National Academy of Sciences USA* that identified two key changes in these genes that dated to at least 200,000 to 100,000 years ago and that honed our ability to fight off pathogens. One change produced a new human variant of the ancestral primate gene *SIGLEC 17*. This variant, however, was nonfunctional. A second event deleted the ancestral gene *SIGLEC 13* entirely. To better understand these changes, Varki and his colleagues experimentally resurrected the proteins once expressed by *SIGLEC 13* and *17*. Both ancestral proteins, they discovered, had been "hacked" by pathogens responsible for two life-threatening infections in babies: group B *Streptococcus* and *E. coli* K1. So as natural selection began weeding out these compromised genes from our genome, the odds of survival rose in human infants.

Such findings add new fuel to the hypothesis that pumped-up immune systems played a key role in lengthening human lives. "Our immune systems went through a lot of changes," Varki says. And as geneticists and biologists continue to investigate the uniquely human part of our genome, many are starting to look for other genetic variants and events that contributed to our long lives today.

Yet already the findings are giving some researchers pause for thought. Public health messages have long warned that lifestyle choices such as couch-potato evenings and calorie-rich diets are largely to blame for the high incidence of atherosclerosis, heart attacks, and strokes. But the new research—particularly the studies on ancient mummies—suggests that the picture may not be quite so simple. Our DNA and an overcharged immune system may well contribute to the development of such diseases. "So maybe we have a little less control over atherosclerosis than we thought," muses cardiologist Thompson. "Maybe our mental framework should be shifted." And perhaps, he adds, researchers should be looking for undiscovered risk factors.

The new findings are also raising a fundamental question about human longevity. Can we, or should we, expect the trend toward longer lives to continue? Some scientists have predicted that babies born after 2000 in countries where life expectancy had already been high–including the United States, Canada, the United Kingdom, and Japan–will live to 100 years of age. Finch is quietly skeptical, however. The emerging trend toward obesity in many human populations and toward environmental deterioration brought about by climate change, he says, could well affect human longevity negatively and throw a major wrench into the works. "I think there is a reason to be cautious about that," Finch concludes. "But time will tell."

Referenced

"Evolution of the Human Lifespan and Diseases of Aging: Roles of Infection, Inflammation, and Nutrition." Caleb E. Finch in Proceedings of the National Academy of Sciences USA, Vol. 107, Supplement No. 1, pages 1718–1724; January 26, 2010.

"Atherosclerosis across 4000 Years of Human History: The Horus Study of Four Ancient Populations." Randall C. Thompson et al. in *Lancet*, Vol. 381, pages 1211–1222; April 2013.

'Computed Tomographic Evidence of Atherosclerosis in the Mummified Remains of Humans from around the World." Randall C. Thompson et al. in *Global Heart*, Vol. 9, No. 2, pages 187–196; June 2014.

About the Author

Heather Pringle is a Canadian science writer and a contributing correspondent for Science.

Aging Is Linked to More Activity in Short Genes Than in Long Genes

By Diana Kwon

Our DNA is made up of genes that vary drastically in size. In humans, genes can be as short as a few hundred molecules known as bases or as long as 2 million bases. These genes carry instructions for constructing proteins and other information crucial to keeping the body running. Now a new study suggests that longer genes become less active than shorter genes as we grow older. And understanding this phenomenon could reveal new ways of countering the aging process.

Luís Amaral, a professor of chemical and biological engineering at Northwestern University, says he and his colleagues did not initially set out to examine gene length. Some of Amaral's collaborators at Northwestern had been trying to pinpoint alterations in gene expression—the process through which the information in a piece of DNA is used to form a functional product, such as a protein or piece of genetic material called RNA—as mice aged. But they were struggling to identify consistent changes. "It seemed like almost everything was random," Amaral says.

Then, at the suggestion of Thomas Stoeger, a postdoctoral scholar in Amaral's lab, the team decided to consider shifts in gene length. Prior studies had hinted that there might be such a large-scale change in gene activity with age—showing, for example, that the amount of RNA declines over time and that disruptions to transcription (the process through which RNA copies, or transcripts, are formed from DNA templates) can have a greater impact on longer genes than shorter ones.

Stoeger, Amaral, and their team used a machine-learning algorithm to identify features that best explained changes in RNA from 17 different tissues, including heart, brain, and kidney, in male mice that were four, nine, 12, 18, and 24 months old. (The strain of mouse used in this study is considered "very old" at 24 months.) This analysis revealed a clear and consistent pattern across tissues: longer transcripts became less abundant than shorter transcripts in older animals. This imbalance in long- and short-gene expression provided a possible explanation for why they couldn't find a specific set of genes whose expression was changing. While the particular genes being expressed varied from experiment to experiment, overall, shorter genes appeared to become more active than longer genes as animals aged, according to Amaral. "You will always find hundreds of genes that seem to change, but once you see it in terms of this linear trend, everything makes sense," he says. (Amaral notes, however, that while changes in transcription are the likeliest explanation for his and his colleagues' findings, other processes, such as the degradation of RNA, may also be at play.)

The team repeated this experiment using data collected from various types of postmortem human tissue, as well as tissues extracted at specific ages in other animals. They found this age-associated imbalance in gene-length-related expression was consistent across organisms. The human findings were particularly exciting, because unlike the mice, which were genetically identical and raised in the same laboratory conditions, the humans lived different lives and died of different causes at different times, Amaral says. "The fact that you find the same pattern despite this diversity really says that this is something robust," he says. "That result dramatically increases my confidence in this being a true and important pattern."

When Amaral and his colleagues looked at the longest and shortest transcripts, they found that the top 5 percent of genes with the shortest transcripts included many linked to shorter lifespans, such as those involved in maintaining the length of telomeres (DNA sequences at the ends of chromosomes that become shorter with age) and immune function. And they found that the top 5 percent of genes with the longest transcripts included ones linked with longevity, such as neuronal activity and transcriptional regulation. They also examined the effects of 12 antiaging interventions on the balance of short- and long-gene activity by reassessing data from previously published animal experiments. Seven of these interventions–which included rapamycin and resveratrol, two antiaging drugs–led to a relative increase in long-gene transcripts, suggesting that this aging-associated imbalance may be reversible. The findings were published in December in *Nature Aging*.

This study fits with previous work, according to Maria Ermolaeva, a group leader at the Leibniz Institute of Aging in Germany, who was not involved in the study. For example, researchers have shown that the accumulation of DNA damage during aging has a stronger effect on longer genes; the longer the gene is, the more likely it is to develop a problem that cannot be repaired, she says. Such unrepaired DNA lesions stall the process of transcription, leading to a reduction in the transcripts produced from longer genes. "The authors of the new study might have observed the global consequences of this previously described molecular phenomenon," Ermolaeva says.

The transcriptome imbalance the authors observe with age "is an interesting association," but whether this process drives aging remains to be seen, says João Pedro de Magalhães, a professor of molecular biogerontology at the University of Birmingham in England, who also was not involved in this study. "I wouldn't discard it as a possibility, but I think you will need some pretty strong evidence that we don't have yet," he says. It could be that length-associated transcriptome changes are simply a reflection of other aging-related processes, such as an uptick in immune system activity. Small genes are often associated with immune function–and immune processes such as inflammation tend to become more active as we get older, de Magalhães adds. "So it makes some sense that you would see patterns in terms of gene length, because it reflects the processes that are being altered with age."

Amaral speculates that the imbalance in transcription could be caused by the accumulation of harmful exposures–viral infections, for example–over the lifespan that gradually alters the cellular machinery required to successfully transcribe longer genes. "Maybe aging is a measure of this imbalance–the greater the imbalance, the more aged you are, the more aged your tissue is," he adds. In future experiments, Amaral hopes to examine how injuries influence the transcriptome imbalance in younger organisms—and to potentially see if antiaging interventions could help restore the imbalance that occurs after potentially damaging exposures.

There are plenty of open questions to address, such as how, exactly, the transcriptional machinery gets altered with age, Amaral says. "We hope that this study will get people excited to do experiments that could help us unravel what's going on in greater depth."

About the Author

Diana Kwon is a freelance journalist who covers health and the life sciences. She is based in Berlin.

Live Long and Proper: Genetic Factors Associated with Increased Longevity Identified

By Nicholette Zeliadt

Have you ever wondered how long you might live? New research suggests that an important indicator of your probable lifespan may be your genes. Scientists have identified unique genetic signatures strongly associated with a long and healthy life, findings that could help to further the understanding of how certain genes may offer protection from common age-related diseases like cancer, dementia, and cardiovascular disease. And one day the data might lead to the development of genetic tests to predict whether a person can expect to live into old age as well as guide intervention efforts to prevent age-related illness.

The study, led by Paola Sebastiani, professor of biostatistics at Boston University (B.U.) School of Public Health, and Thomas Perls, professor of medicine and geriatrics at the B.U. School of Medicine, was published online July 1 in *Science*.

A person's lifespan is thought to be largely determined by the combined effects of genetics and environmental factors. Twin studies, however, suggest genetics only account for approximately 20 to 30 percent of an individual's chance of surviving to age 85.

Lifestyle choices, particularly diet, exercise, and smoking habits, play an undisputed role in determining not only how long one will live but also how well one ages. Studies show that Seventh-Day Adventists, whose church encourages behaviors that promote healthy aging, have a well-documented average lifespan of 88 years, approximately eight years longer than the average U.S. citizen. For the most part, Adventists exercise regularly, are vegetarian, and don't smoke or drink alcohol.

Nevertheless, a glance at your family tree may indicate whether you have a familial tendency toward longevity. Research suggests that exceptional longevity (EL)–living one to three decades beyond the average U.S. lifespan of approximately 80 years–runs strongly in families. "That...has always made us believe that genetics is playing a very important role in this wonderful trait," Perls said in a press conference.

Genetic factors can contribute to the degree of longevity in at least two important ways: An individual may inherit certain genetic variations that predispose him or her to disease that decreases longevity; other gene variants may confer disease resistance, thereby increasing it.

To better understand the genetic components of longevity, the researchers analyzed the DNA of more than 800 subjects between the ages of 95 to 119 and compared it with DNA from random controls. The genome-wide survey identified specific genetic variations, or SNPs (single-nucleotide polymorphisms), that were associated with the longevity group.

Next, the researchers developed a genetic model comprising 150 SNPs in order to compute the predisposition of an individual toward EL. Their model successfully predicted exceptional longevity in a different sample of centenarians (individuals that live to age 100) with 77 percent accuracy. This demonstrates that EL is strongly associated with complex combinations of genetic variants.

The researchers found that, based on subjects' genetic profiles, the centenarians could be further divided into 19 subgroups, some of which were associated with delayed onset of age-related diseases such as dementia, hypertension, and cardiovascular disease. These signatures represent different genetic paths to age 100 and beyond, Sebastiani said in the press conference.

"Centenarians are indeed a model of aging well," Perls said. Previous work has shown that 90 percent of centenarians are disability-free at the age of 93. In industrialized nations approximately one out of every 6,000 people lives beyond the age of 100. Supercentenarians, or individuals that are older than 110, are even rarer–only one in 7 million fall into this category.

Surprisingly, the researchers found that approximately 15 percent of control subjects also had the genetic signature associated with longevity. This suggests that many more people have the genetic potential to survive into old age than previously thought. "We know a lot about the human genome, but we also know that there is a lot that remains to be discovered," Sebastiani said. "Genetics is fundamental in EL, but it's not the only thing. So there may be other factors like environment or other lifestyles that may help people live longer and healthier lives," he added.

Importantly, there was no difference in the presence of known disease-associated gene variants between the longevity and control groups. The researchers conclude that EL may result from an enrichment of longevity-associated gene variants that may counteract the effects of having a disease-associated gene.

"I think this is a step towards making sense out of a lot of data–genetic data, environmental data, epidemiological data–to help us understand factors that contribute to long and healthy life," says Winifred Rossi, deputy director of the Division of Geriatrics and Clinical Gerontology at the National Institute on Aging, who wasn't involved in the study.

"We're starting to get to the point where it might be possible to use the information about these variants to predict someone's likelihood of achieving EL," says Matt Kaeberlein, professor of pathology at the University of Washington in Seattle, also not involved in the study. He added that the challenge was to next move beyond this correlative study to figure out how these gene variations may lead to functional changes that contribute to the molecular process of aging.

The authors caution that further study and replication of their results in different populations is needed to verify their model before it will be useful for individual genetic tests–or before longevity "cocktails" are created.

"My hope has always been with the study that we would learn much more about how to get lots of people to live to older age in good health and markedly delay their disability and age of onset of diseases...," Perls said. "I look at the complexity of this puzzle and feel very strongly that this will not lead to treatments that will get a lot of people to become centenarians, but rather will make a dent in the onset of age-related diseases like Alzheimer's, for example."

Section 2: Death and the Mind

What Near-Death Experiences Reveal about the Brain

By Christof Koch

A young Ernest Hemingway, badly injured by an exploding shell on a World War I battlefield, wrote in a letter home that "dying is a very simple thing. I've looked at death, and really I know. If I should have died it would have been very easy for me. Quite the easiest thing I ever did."

Years later Hemingway adapted his own experience–that of the soul leaving the body, taking flight, and then returning–for his famous short story "The Snows of Kilimanjaro," about an African safari gone disastrously wrong. The protagonist, stricken by gangrene, knows he is dying. Suddenly, his pain vanishes, and Compie, a bush pilot, arrives to rescue him. The two take off and fly together through a storm with rain so thick "it seemed like flying through a waterfall" until the plane emerges into the light: before them, "unbelievably white in the sun, was the square top of Kilimanjaro. And then he knew that there was where he was going." The description embraces elements of a classic near-death experience: the darkness, the cessation of pain, the emerging into the light, and then a feeling of peacefulness.

Peace Beyond Understanding

Near-death experiences, or NDEs, are triggered during singular life-threatening episodes when the body is injured by blunt trauma, a heart attack, asphyxia, shock, and so on. About one in 10 patients with cardiac arrest in a hospital setting undergoes such an episode. Thousands of survivors of these harrowing touch-and-go situations tell of leaving their damaged bodies behind and encountering a realm beyond everyday existence, unconstrained by the usual boundaries of space and time. These powerful, mystical experiences can lead to permanent transformation of their lives.

NDEs are not fancy flights of the imagination. They share broad commonalities–becoming pain-free, seeing a bright light at the end of a tunnel and other visual phenomena, detaching from one's body and floating above it, or even flying off into space (out-of-body experiences). They might include meeting loved ones, living or dead, or spiritual beings such as angels; a Proustian recollection or even review of lifetime memories, both good and bad ("my life flashed in front of my eyes"); or a distorted sense of time and space. There are some underlying physiological explanations for these perceptions, such as progressively narrowing tunnel vision. Reduced blood flow to the visual periphery of the retina means vision loss occurs there first.

NDEs can be either positive or negative experiences. The former receive all the press and relate to the feeling of an overwhelming presence, something numinous, divine. A jarring disconnect separates the massive trauma to the body and the peacefulness and feeling of oneness with the universe. Yet not all NDEs are blissful–some can be frightening, marked by intense terror, anguish, loneliness, and despair.

It is likely that the publicity around NDEs has built up expectations about what people should feel after such episodes. It seems possible, in fact, that distressing NDEs are significantly underreported because of shame, social stigma, and pressure to conform to the prototype of the "blissful" NDE.

Any close brush with death reminds us of the precariousness and fragility of life and can strip away the layers of psychological suppression that shield us from uncomfortable thoughts of existential oblivion. For most, these events fade in intensity with time, and normality eventually reasserts itself (although they may leave post-traumatic stress disorder in their wake). But NDEs are recalled with unusual intensity and lucidity over decades.

A 2017 study by two researchers at the University of Virginia raised the question of whether the paradox of enhanced cognition occurring alongside compromised brain function during an NDE could be written off as a flight of imagination. The researchers administered a questionnaire to 122 people who reported NDEs. They asked them to compare memories of their experiences with those of both real and imagined events from about the same time. The results suggest that the NDEs were recalled with greater vividness and detail than either real or imagined situations were. In short, the NDEs were remembered as being "realer than real."

NDEs came to the attention of the general public in the last quarter of the 20th century from the work of physicians and psychologists–in particular Raymond Moody, who coined the term "near-death experience" in his 1975 best seller, *Life after Life*, and Bruce M. Greyson, one of the two researchers on the study mentioned earlier, who also published *The Handbook of Near-Death Experiences* in 2009. Noticing patterns in what people would share about their near-death stories, these researchers turned a phenomenon once derided as confabulation or dismissed as feverish hallucination (deathbed visions of yore) into a field of empirical study.

I accept the reality of these intensely felt experiences. They are as authentic as any other subjective feeling or perception. As a scientist, however, I operate under the hypothesis that all our thoughts, memories, percepts, and experiences are an ineluctable consequence of the natural causal powers of our brain rather than of any supernatural ones. That premise has served science and its handmaiden, technology, extremely well over the past few centuries. Unless there is extraordinary, compelling, objective evidence to the contrary, I see no reason to abandon this assumption.

The challenge, then, is to explain NDEs within a natural framework. As a longtime student of the mind-body problem, I care about NDEs because they constitute a rare variety of human consciousness and because of the remarkable fact that an event lasting well under an hour in objective time leaves a permanent transformation in its wake, a Pauline conversion on the road to Damascus–no more fear of death, a detachment from material possessions and an orientation toward the greater good. Or, as in the case of Hemingway, an obsession with risk and death.

Similar mystical experiences are commonly reported when ingesting psychoactive substances from a class of hallucinogens linked to the neurotransmitter serotonin, including psilocybin (the active ingredient in magic mushrooms), LSD, DMT (aka the Spirit Molecule), and 5-MeO-DMT (aka the God Molecule), consumed as part of religious, spiritual, or recreational practices.

The Undiscovered Country

It must be remembered that NDEs have been with us at all times in all cultures and in all people, young and old, devout and skeptical (think, for instance, of the so-called *Tibetan Book of the Dead*, which describes the mind before and after death). To those raised in religious traditions, Christian or otherwise, the most obvious explanation is that they were granted a vision of heaven or hell, of what awaits them in the hereafter. Interestingly, NDEs are no more likely to occur in devout believers than in secular or nonpracticing subjects.

Personal narratives drawn from the historical record furnish intensely vivid accounts of NDEs that can be as instructive as any dry, clinical case report, if not more so. In 1791, for instance, British admiral Sir Francis Beaufort (after whom the Beaufort wind scale is named) almost drowned, an event he recalled in this fashion:

> Local brain regions go offline one after another. The mind, whose substrate is whichever neurons remain intact, then does what it always does: it tells a story shaped by a person's experience, memory and cultural expectations.
>
> A calm feeling of the most perfect tranquility succeeded the most tumultuous sensation.... Nor was I in any bodily pain. On the contrary, my sensations were now of rather a pleasurable cast .... Though the senses were thus deadened, not so the mind; its activity seemed to be invigorated in a ratio which defies all description; for thought rose after thought with a rapidity of succession that

> is not only indescribable, but probably inconceivable, by anyone who has been himself in a similar situation. The course of these thoughts I can even now in a great measure retrace: the event that had just taken place .... Thus, traveling backwards, every incident of my past life seemed to me to glance across my recollection in retrograde procession ... the whole period of my existence seemed to be placed before me in a kind of panoramic view.

Another instance was recorded in 1900, when Scottish surgeon Sir Alexander Ogston (discoverer of *Staphylococcus*) succumbed to a bout of typhoid fever. He described what happened this way:

> I lay, as it seemed, in a constant stupor which excluded the existence of any hopes or fears. Mind and body seemed to be dual, and to some extent separate. I was conscious of the body as an inert tumbled mass near a door; it belonged to me, but it was not I. I was conscious that my mental self used regularly to leave the body .... I was then drawn rapidly back to it, joined it with disgust, and it became I, and was fed, spoken to, and cared for .... And though I knew that death was hovering about, having no thought of religion nor dread of the end, and roamed on beneath the murky skies apathetic and contented until something again disturbed the body where it lay, when I was drawn back to it afresh.

More recently, British writer Susan Blackmore received a report from a woman from Cyprus who had an emergency gastrectomy in 1991:

> On the fourth day following that operation I went into shock and became unconscious for several hours .... Although thought to be unconscious, I remembered, for years afterwards, the entire, detailed conversation that passed between the surgeon and anaesthetist present .... I was lying above my own body, totally free of pain, and looking down at my own self with compassion for the agony I could see on the face; I was floating peacefully. Then ... I was going elsewhere, floating towards a dark, but not frightening, curtain-like area ... Then I felt total peace. Suddenly it all changed–I was slammed back into my body again, very much aware of the agony again.

The underlying neurological sequence of events in a near-death experience is difficult to determine with any precision because of the dizzying variety of ways in which the brain can be damaged. Furthermore, NDEs do not strike when the individual is lying inside a magnetic scanner or has their scalp covered by a net of electrodes.

It is possible, though, to gain some idea of what happens by examining a cardiac arrest, in which the heart stops beating (the patient is "coding," in hospital jargon). The patient has not died, because the heart can be jump-started via cardiopulmonary resuscitation.

Modern death requires irreversible loss of brain function. When the brain is starved of blood flow (ischemia) and oxygen (anoxia), the patient faints in a fraction of a minute and their electroencephalogram, or EEG, becomes isoelectric–in other words, flat. This implies that large-scale, spatially distributed electrical activity within the cortex, the outermost layer of the brain, has broken down. Like a town that loses power one neighborhood at a time, local regions of the brain go offline one after another. The mind, whose substrate is whichever neurons remain capable of generating electrical activity, does what it always does: it tells a story shaped by the person's experience, memory, and cultural expectations.

Given these power outages, this experience may produce the rather strange and idiosyncratic stories that make up the corpus of NDE reports. To the person undergoing it, the NDE is as real as anything the mind produces during normal waking. When the entire brain has shut down because of complete power loss, the mind is extinguished, along with consciousness. If and when oxygen and blood flow are restored, the brain boots up, and the narrative flow of experience resumes.

Scientists have videotaped, analyzed, and dissected the loss and subsequent recovery of consciousness in highly trained individuals–U.S. test pilots and NASA astronauts in centrifuges during the Cold War (recall the scene in the 2018 movie *First Man* of a stoic Neil Armstrong, played by Ryan Gosling, being spun in a multiaxis trainer until he passes out). At around five times the force of gravity, the cardiovascular system stops delivering blood to the brain, and the pilot faints. About 10 to 20 seconds after these large g-forces cease, consciousness returns, accompanied by a comparable interval of confusion and disorientation (subjects in these tests are obviously very fit and pride themselves on their self-control).

The range of phenomena these men recount may amount to "NDE lite"–tunnel vision and bright lights; a feeling of awakening from sleep, including partial or complete paralysis; a sense of peaceful floating; out-of-body experiences; sensations of pleasure and even euphoria; and short but intense dreams, often involving conversations with family members, that remain vivid to them many years afterward. These intensely felt experiences, triggered by a specific physical insult, typically do not have any religious character (perhaps because participants knew ahead of time that they would be stressed until they fainted).

By their very nature, NDEs are not readily amenable to well-controlled laboratory experimentation, although this might change. For instance, it may be possible to study aspects of them in the humble lab mouse–maybe it, too, can experience a review of lifetime memories or euphoria before death.

The Fading of the Light

Many neurologists have noted similarities between NDEs and the effects of a class of epileptic events known as complex partial seizures. These fits partially impair consciousness and often are localized to specific brain regions in one hemisphere. They can be preceded by an aura, which is a specific experience unique to an individual patient that is predictive of an incipient attack. The seizure may be accompanied by changes in the perceived sizes of objects; unusual tastes, smells, or bodily feelings; déjà vu; depersonalization; or ecstatic feelings. Episodes featuring the last items on this list are also clinically known as Dostoyevsky's seizures, after the late 19th-century Russian writer Fyodor Dostoyevsky, who suffered from severe temporal lobe epilepsy. Prince Myshkin, the protagonist of his novel *The Idiot*, remembers:

> During his epileptic fits, or rather immediately preceding them, he had always experienced a moment or two when his whole heart, and mind, and body seemed to wake up to vigor and light; when he became filled with joy and hope, and all his anxieties seemed to be swept away forever; these moments were but presentiments, as it were, of the one final second (it was never more than a second) in which the fit came upon him. That second, of course, was inexpressible. When his attack was over, and the prince reflected on his symptoms, he used to say to himself: ... "What matter though it be only disease, an abnormal tension of the brain, if when I recall and analyze the moment, it seems to have been one of harmony and beauty in the highest degree—an instant of deepest sensation, overflowing with unbounded joy and rapture, ecstatic devotion, and completest life? ... I would give my whole life for this one instant.

More than 150 years later neurosurgeons are able to induce such ecstatic feelings by electrically stimulating part of the cortex called the insula in epileptic patients who have electrodes implanted in their brain. This procedure can help locate the origin of the seizures for possible surgical removal. Patients report bliss, enhanced well-being, and heightened self-awareness or perception of the external world. Exciting the gray matter elsewhere can trigger out-of-body experiences or visual hallucinations. This brute link between abnormal activity patterns—whether induced by the spontaneous disease process or controlled by a surgeon's electrode—and subjective experience provides support for a biological, not spiritual, origin. The same is likely to be true for NDEs.

Why the mind should experience the struggle to sustain its operations in the face of loss of blood flow and oxygen as positive and blissful rather than as panic-inducing remains mysterious. It is intriguing, though, that the outer limit of the spectrum of human experience encompasses other occasions in which reduced oxygen causes pleasurable feelings of jauntiness, light-headedness, and heightened arousal—deepwater diving, high-altitude climbing, flying, the choking or fainting game, and sexual asphyxiation.

Perhaps such ecstatic experiences are common to many forms of death as long as the mind remains lucid and is not dulled by opiates or other drugs given to alleviate pain. The mind, chained to a dying body, visits its own private version of heaven or hell before entering Hamlet's "undiscovered country from whose bourn no traveler returns."

Referenced

The Handbook of Near-Death Experiences: Thirty Years of Investigation. Edited by Janice Miner Holden, Bruce Greyson and Debbie James. Praeger, 2009.

"Leaving Body and Life Behind: Out-of-Body and Near-Death Experience." Olaf Blanke, Nathan Faivre and Sebastian Dieguez in *The Neurology of Consciousness*. Second edition. Edited by Steven Laureys, Olivia Gosseries and Giulio Tononi. Academic Press, 2015.

About the Author

Christof Koch is a neuroscientist at the Allen Institute and at the Tiny Blue Dot Foundation, the former president of the Allen Institute for Brain Science, and a former professor at the California Institute of Technology. His latest book is Then I Am Myself the World. *Koch writes regularly for a range of media, including* Scientific American. *He lives in the Pacific Northwest.*

Lifting the Veil on Near-Death Experiences

By Rachel Nuwer

For decades François D'Adesky, a retired diplomat and civil servant who now lives in Brussels, spoke to no one about his near-death experience (NDE). It happened at the age of 13, when he was hospitalized for acute appendicitis. D'Adesky vividly recalls seeing his body on the operating table and then passing through a tunnel, where he met strange beings who radiated luminosity and goodness. "Your time has not come," an older being, who D'Adesky intuited was God, told him. "You have not undertaken your Earth mission."

Then D'Adesky perceived traveling "at breakneck speed through time and space, back to the beginning of the creation of the world," he says. He eventually arrived at a gardenlike paradise where spiritual beings–one of whom was his deceased grandmother, another a childhood friend who had died at the age of five–communicated telepathically with him. D'Adesky's grandmother took him by the hand and led him back into the clinic, where he woke up in his body in excruciating pain.

D'Adesky spent his adult life striving to discover what his special mission was. Eventually he came to see it as the role he played in "making the world a better place," he says. That included helping, as an official with the United Nations, to get a key resolution passed at the 2011 U.N. Climate Change Conference. It wasn't until a few years later, though, when NDEs were entering the public discourse more often, that he started sharing the story of his pivotal experience beyond his immediate family. "I had been afraid for my reputation," he says.

Near-death experiences have been reported across time and cultures. An astounding 5 to 10 percent of the general population is estimated to have memories of an NDE, including somewhere between 10 and 23 percent of cardiac arrest survivors. A growing number of scholars now accept NDEs as a unique mental state that can offer novel insights into the nature of consciousness. "Now, clearly, we don't question anymore the reality of near-death experiences," says Charlotte Martial, a neuroscientist at the University of Liège in Belgium. "People who report an experience really did experience something."

Those who undergo an NDE also return with "this noetic quality from the experience, which very often changes their life," adds neuroscientist Christof Koch of the Allen Institute in Seattle, who writes about NDEs and other states of consciousness in his 2024 book, *Then I Am Myself the World*. "They know what they've seen."

A handful of researchers, mostly emergency room doctors, began collecting qualitative data about NDEs after the 1975 publication of psychiatrist and physician Raymond A. Moody's book *Life after Life*, which detailed patients' accounts of near-death experiences. Since then, only a few research teams have attempted to empirically investigate the neurobiology of NDEs. But their findings are already challenging long-held beliefs about the dying brain, including that consciousness ceases almost immediately after the heart stops beating. This discovery has important implications for current resuscitation practices, which are based on outdated beliefs about what happens to the brain during cardiac arrest, says neuroscientist Jimo Borjigin of the University of Michigan Medical School. "If we understand the mechanisms of death, then this could lead to new ways of saving lives."

Like psychedelic drugs and other means of altering consciousness, NDEs could also serve as probes for revealing fundamental truths about the mind and brain. Such states are perturbations to the system of consciousness, "and when you perturb a system, you understand better how it works," says Christopher Timmermann, a postdoctoral fellow at the Center for Psychedelic Research at Imperial College London. "If we want to understand the nature of experience, we have to take into account what's happening at the margins of nonordinary states."

Moreover, there are important existential implications, although exactly what those might be continues to be debated in the scientific literature and at conferences, including at a 2023 meeting held by the New York Academy of Sciences. It explored consciousness through the lens of death, psychedelics, and mysticism. "These transcendent experiences are found in the major world religions and traditions," says Anthony Bossis, a clinical assistant professor of psychiatry at the New York University Grossman School of Medicine, who helped to organize the conference. "Might they have some greater purpose for helping humanity cultivate understanding and awareness of consciousness?" he asks. The weightiness of such questions makes careful study of NDEs and their rigorous interpretation all the more critical, Martial says: "It's important to disentangle empirical findings versus belief."

On an overcast February afternoon, Martial was meeting with the 20 members of her neuroscience laboratory when her phone began to ring. She had asked to be alerted if someone arrived at the Liège university hospital on the verge of death.

Martial bolted toward the elevator, and within about two minutes she made it into the hospital lobby, its crisscrossing escalators and geometric motifs reminiscent of an M. C. Escher drawing. In the resuscitation room, Aurore Ancion, an emergency physician and doctoral candidate in medical sciences, was already waiting. Laid out on one of the room's two beds was a bearded man in his mid-70s, his hospital gown open to expose his belly and chest.

Despite being in the middle of an episode of atrial fibrillation, the man was alert and cracking jokes. He giggled nervously as Ancion, working around two other emergency doctors, placed a cap over his head for an electroencephalogram (or EEG, to measure electrical signals in the brain) and adhered two oxygen readers to his forehead. Martial, standing in the back, peered through tortoiseshell glasses at a laptop, where two spiky lines in red and blue began scrolling across the screen—precise measurements, to the trained eye, of the patient's brain activity.

The doctors eventually had to anesthetize the man and shock his heart back into a normal rhythm. Martial and her colleagues hope the data from his and other patients' visits to the resuscitation room and from follow-up interviews will provide the most detailed picture to date of what transpires in the human brain during close encounters with death.

Many people who had an NDE describe one or more of a specific set of characteristics. They may recall separating from their body and viewing it in real time from above. They may pass through tunnels and see light, encounter deceased relatives or compassionate entities, and have a sense of vastness and deep insight. People may undergo a life review and morally evaluate the choices they have made, including by experiencing the joy or pain their actions caused others. "What's intriguing is that when people die, they don't evaluate themselves based on their own standards of morals," says Sam Parnia, director of critical care and resuscitation research at the N.Y.U. Langone medical center. "They evaluate themselves based on a universal standard."

Although most people describe their NDE in glowing terms, a minority recount visits to hell-like regions, encounters with demonic beings or terrifying voids. In a 2019 study, Martial and her colleagues found that among 123 people who reported an NDE, 14 percent classified it as negative—a proportion Martial says she's "sure" is an underestimate because of how disturbing these memories can be.

Somewhat surprisingly, religious people don't seem to be more inclined toward NDEs. There is, however, preliminary evidence of another group being more likely to have NDEs: those who are prone to REM sleep intrusion, a condition that occurs when rapid eye movement (REM) sleep intrudes into wakefulness and blends elements of dreaming and waking. During the seconds or minutes it lasts for, people may have an out-of-body experience, sense that someone or something is in the room with them, or want to move but find that they can't. In 2019 Daniel Kondziella, a neurologist at the Copenhagen University Hospital network's Rigshospitalet, and his colleagues recruited a sample of 1,034 adults from the general population in 35 countries. Ten percent of the study participants had experienced an NDE, and of those, 47 percent also reported REM sleep intrusion—a statistically significant association. Among the people who had not had NDEs, just 14 percent reported REM sleep intrusion.

Still, little is known about the neurobiology of NDEs. Open questions include whether they are driven by a single, core mechanism or are a more variable response to "understanding somehow that death is near," as Timmermann says. A few researchers, including Martial, are peering into the brains of people who are approaching or undergoing death, in the hope of understanding what is going on.

In 2023 Borjigin and her colleagues published what they suspect could be a signature of NDEs in the dying brain. The researchers analyzed EEG data from four comatose patients before and after their ventilators were removed. As their brains became deprived of oxygen, two of the dying patients exhibited a paradoxical surge of gamma activity, a type of high-frequency brain wave linked to the formation of memory and the integration of information.

Borjigin had seen the same upwelling of activity in previous studies of the brains of healthy rats during induced cardiac arrest. In the rodents, the surge occurred across the entire brain. In humans, though, it was confined primarily to the junction of the brain's temporal, parietal and occipital lobes, a region involved in multiple features of consciousness, including visual, auditory, and motion processing. Past research has also associated the region with out-of-body sensations, as well as with altruism and empathy. Although these are all regular components of NDEs, Borjigin says, it's impossible to know whether the two patients actually experienced an NDE because they did not live to tell about it. But "I could almost guess what they might have experienced," she says.

A 2023 study led by Parnia and detailed in his 2024 book, *Lucid Dying*, provides further evidence of brain activity after patients' hearts have stopped. Parnia and his colleagues worked with 25 hospitals in the United States, the United Kingdom, and Bulgaria to review EEG and brain-oxygen data from 567 people who experienced an in-hospital cardiac arrest. Medical staff managed to collect interpretable EEG data from 53 of these patients. Most showed an electrical flatline during the crisis, but in around 40 percent of those cases, neurological activity consistent with that of conscious brains transiently reemerged—in some instances up to an hour into CPR.

A different subset of 53 patients from the study survived. Doctors collected EEG and brain-oxygen levels for too few of these people to draw a correlation between any potential memory they had of the event and their brain activity. The authors were able to interview 28 of the survivors, and six had a "recalled experience of death," as Parnia refers to NDEs.

Parnia and his colleagues also sought to test conscious and unconscious awareness, including reports of out-of-body experiences, by projecting a series of 10 random images on a tablet placed near patients' heads and by playing a repeated recording of the names of three fruits—apple, pear, banana—to them through headphones every minute for five minutes while they were unconscious. None of the survivors could remember the images that had been projected. One person who had a recalled experience of death correctly named the fruits in order, although this could have been by chance, Parnia says.

According to Parnia, this study presents "a coherent, mechanistic explanation" for how and why people have recalled experiences of death. When someone starts dying, Parnia says, the brain becomes dysfunctional. Some actions are immediately lost, such as brain stem reflexes, but others that are normally suppressed to optimize performance for ordinary life suddenly become disinhibited because the brain's natural braking systems are no longer working. As a result, "your entire consciousness comes to the fore," Parnia says. The purpose of this change, he suggests, is to prepare the person "for a new reality"—the transition from life to death, a condition in which, Parnia believes, consciousness endures.

Other scientists flatly disagree. "When you have an NDE, you must have a functioning brain to store the memory, and you have to survive with an intact brain so you can retrieve that memory and tell about it," Kondziella says. "You can't do that without a functioning brain, so all those arguments that NDEs prove that there's consciousness outside the brain are simply nonsense."

Kondziella, Martial, and others instead theorize that NDEs might be part of a last-ditch survival tactic. Species across the animal kingdom "play dead"–a behavior technically called thanatosis–when they perceive a mortal threat, typically from an attacking predator. If fight-or-flight fails, the instinct to feign death kicks in as an attempt to forestall the danger. The animal becomes immobilized and unresponsive to external stimuli–but with continued awareness so that, given a chance, it can escape. "Personally, I believe the evolutionary aspect really is the key to understanding what NDEs are and how they came about," Kondziella says. "There is a perfectly valid biological explanation."

Martial and others have also criticized the methodological rigor of Parnia's study. One concern, Martial says, is that the team based its findings on visual readings of patients' EEGs rather than on "a proper statistical analysis." Parnia says he and his colleagues applied the standard method for reading EEGs that "every physician in the world" uses in clinical practice. Those who are criticizing the study, he adds, are "just ignoring it because [they] don't like it."

In their latest study, Martial and her colleagues plan to use the most rigorous approach to date to collect both subjective and objective data from around 100 patients, including EEG and brain-oxygen readings, plus information from several rounds of interviews and surveys with survivors in the group. The University of Liège team is also trying to more thoroughly evaluate claims about out-of-body experiences. Around 79 percent of people who have an NDE report leaving their body, and some wake up knowing facts about their environment that they seemingly should not know. "I'm not saying it's not true, but here we want to objectively test it," Martial says.

To this end, she and her colleagues have decorated the hospital resuscitation room with unexpected objects and images, some of which are hidden in places that could be viewed only from the vantage point of someone near the ceiling. While a patient is in the resuscitation room, including while they are conscious, the team plays an audio clip of various words and animal sounds once every minute. They will test for recollections of any images or sounds in follow-ups with surviving participants, and they will also use video recordings to compare people's memories with reality.

An easier approach to studying NDEs is via safe proxies such as hypnosis, induced fainting and psychedelic drugs. None of these methods produce true NDEs, but the states they trigger may have some overlap with the dying brain. In 2018 Timmermann, Martial and their colleagues published a study comparing NDEs with the effects of *N,N*-dimethyltryptamine (DMT), a mind-altering component of ayahuasca, a South American plant-derived psychedelic brew. Trace amounts of DMT also occur endogenously in humans. "There's speculation that that's somehow underlying NDEs, but the data are very elementary," Timmermann says.

In the study, 13 volunteers received intravenous DMT in a lab setting and rated their experience on a scale commonly used to measure NDEs, as developed by psychiatrist Bruce Greyson in 1983. The researchers compared the DMT group's scores and subjective accounts with other people's taken from an NDE database that Martial and her colleagues have been compiling since 2016. (The database includes around 2,000 accounts, accepted from anyone who contacts the Liège team claiming to have had an NDE and then fills out a lengthy questionnaire.)

They found "striking overlap" between the DMT and NDE groups, Martial says, with people in both describing a sense of entering into an unearthly realm, separating from their body, encountering mystical beings, and seeing a bright light. People in both groups also reported feelings of peace, unity, and joy. There was just one significant difference: those in the NDE group more frequently experienced reaching a border demarcating a point of no return.

Roland Griffiths, a psychiatrist at Johns Hopkins University who pioneered studies of psilocybin and who died last October, reported similar findings with his colleagues in 2022. The authors compared 3,192 people who had undergone an NDE, a psychedelic drug trip, or a nondrug-induced mystical experience. The team found "remarkably similar" long-term outcomes across subjects in all three groups, including a reduced fear of death and lasting positive effects of insights they had gained.

In another study, published in 2024 in the journal *Neuroscience of Consciousness*, Martial, Timmermann and their colleagues interviewed 31 people who had experienced an NDE and had also tried a psychedelic drug–LSD, psilocybin, ayahuasca, DMT, or mescaline–to see what they had to say about the similarities and differences between the events. Participants reported stronger sensory effects during their NDE, including the sensation of being disembodied, but stronger visual imagery during their drug trip. They reported feelings of spirituality, connectedness, and deeper meaning across both.

In comparisons of these mystical experiences, "the common ground that's striking to me is in things like a profound, deep sense of love–that all is love and that consciousness is love," says Bossis, who studies the effects of psilocybin in people with terminal cancer, focusing on relieving end-of-life distress, enhancing spirituality, and providing a greater sense of meaning and fulfillment in life. "There's also a sense of transcending time as we know it and a greater acceptance of the mystery of life and death."

To Guy Vander Linden, a retired government administrator in Brussels, his NDE is still a "gift." It happened in 1990 after a serious bike accident. He was enveloped by a force of overwhelming love and a deep sense of "spirituality not connected to religion," he says. He also felt an expansiveness in which "I was everything and nothing."

Vander Linden left the hospital a different person. His fear of death was extinguished, he says, because he now knew that "to die is something fantastic." He no longer saw value in material things and got rid of his car and two extra houses. He also felt compelled to share his NDE with others through books and conferences. These changes affected his relationships, including with his wife, whom he has since divorced. "She said I'm crazy," Vander Linden recalls. "To come back with an experience that others haven't had–it creates conflict." Years later he is still able to tap into the love he felt when he was bathed in the clear light of what he's come to conceive of as universal consciousness.

Regardless of how people interpret NDEs, studying them may expand the boundaries of resuscitation, provide a better understanding of mind and brain, and shine a flicker of light on some of the deepest mysteries of existence.

About the Author

Rachel Nuwer is a science journalist and author. Her latest book is I Feel Love: MDMA and the Quest for Connection in a Fractured World *(Bloomsbury, 2023). Follow her on X @RachelNuwer.*

Some Patients Who 'Died' but Survived Report Lucid 'Near-Death Experiences,' a New Study Shows

By Rachel Nuwer

What happens when we actually die—when our heart stops and all electrical activity "flatlines" in our brain?

Humans have been asking this question since time immemorial. It's a tough one because the dead do not normally ping back to us about the nature of their experiences. Religious texts are capable of supplying a multitude of explanations. But scientists have not given up on providing their own set of answers, and they are making some strides in better understanding the brain's process of transitioning from life to death.

Most recently, this has become possible because of research that has monitored the brains of people who have been in the throes of actually dying. Some of these individuals have been able to report back about what they experienced. According to findings published on September 14 in *Resuscitation*, the flatlined brains of some cardiac arrest patients burst into a flurry of activity during CPR, even though their heart stopped beating up to an hour. A small subset of study participants who survived were able to recall the experience, and one person was able to identify an audio stimulus that was played while doctors were trying to resuscitate them.

The researchers interpret the brain recordings they made of these patients as markers of "lucid, recalled experiences of death"—an observation that has "never been possible before," says lead author Sam Parnia, an associate professor of medicine at NYU Langone Health and a longtime researcher of what happens to people as they die. "We've also been able to put forward a coherent, mechanistic explanation for why this occurs."

"Recalled experiences of death"—a term Parnia prefers over "near-death experiences" for accuracy—have been reported across diverse cultures throughout recorded history. Some Western scientists previously dismissed such stories as hallucinations or dreams, but recently a few research teams have begun to pay more serious attention to the phenomena as a means to investigate consciousness and shine light on the mysteries of death.

In the new study, Parnia and his colleagues sought to find a biological signature of recalled experiences of death. They teamed up with 25 hospitals, primarily in the United States and the United Kingdom. Medical personnel used portable devices that could be placed on the heads of patients who were having a cardiac emergency to measure their brain oxygen levels and electrical activity without interfering with their medical treatment. The researchers also tested for conscious and unconscious perceptions by placing headphones on patients that played a repeated recording of the names of three fruits: banana, pear, and apple. In terms of unconscious learning, a person who does not remember hearing these fruit names but is asked to "randomly think of three fruits" may still give the right answer, Parnia says. Past research has shown, for example, that even people in a deep coma can unconsciously learn the names of fruits or cities if those words are whispered in their ear.

Between May 2017 and March 2020, 567 people suffered cardiac arrests at participating hospitals. Medical staff managed to gather usable brain oxygen and activity data from 53 of these patients, most of whom showed an electrical flatline state on electroencephalographic (EEG) brain monitors. But about 40 percent then experienced electrical activity that reemerged at some point with normal to near-normal brain waves that were consistent with consciousness. This activity was sometimes restored up to 60 minutes into CPR.

Of the 567 total patients, just 53 survived. The researchers conducted interviews with 28 of the survivors. They also interviewed 126 people from the community who had gone through cardiac arrests because the sample size of survivors from the new study was so small. Nearly 40 percent reported some perceived awareness of the event without specific memories attached, and 20 percent seemed to have had a recalled experience of death. Many in the latter group described the event as a "moral evaluation" of "their entire life and how they've conducted themselves," Parnia says.

In their interviews with survivors, the researchers found that just one person was able to recall the names of fruits that had been played while they received CPR. Parnia acknowledges that this individual could have guessed the correct fruits by chance.

He and his colleagues have developed a working hypothesis to explain their findings. Normally, the brain has "braking systems" in place that filter most elements of brain function out of our experience of consciousness. This enables people to efficiently operate in the world, because under regular circumstances, "you couldn't function with access to your whole brain's activity being in the realm of consciousness," he says.

In the dying brain, however, the researchers hypothesize that the braking system is removed. Parts that are normally dormant become active, and the dying person gains access to their entire consciousness–"all your thoughts, all your memories, everything that's been stored before," Parnia says. "We don't know the evolutionary benefit of this, but it seems to prepare people for their transition from life into death."

The findings also raise questions about the brain's resiliency to oxygen deprivation. It could be, Parnia says, that some people who have conventionally been thought to be beyond the point of saving could in fact be revived. "The traditional thinking among doctors is that the brain, once deprived of oxygen for five to 10 minutes, dies," he says. "We were able to show that the brain is quite robust in terms of its ability to resist oxygen deprivation for prolonged periods of time, which opens up new pathways for finding treatments for brain damage in the future."

The new study "represents a Herculean effort to understand as objectively as possible the nature of brain function as it may apply to consciousness and near-death experiences during cardiac arrest," says Lakhmir Chawla, an intensive care unit physician at Jennifer Moreno Department of Veterans Affairs Medical Center in San Diego, Calif., who was not involved in the research but has published papers on spikes of EEG activity at the time of death in some patients.

While the results Parnia and his colleagues report are "striking" from a scientific point of view, "I believe that we should allow these data to also inform our humanity," he adds. For one, the findings should "compel clinicians to treat patients who are receiving CPR as if they are awake," which is something "we rarely do."

And for those individuals who do seem to be beyond saving, Chawla says, doctors could invite their families in to come say goodbye, "as the patient may still be able to hear them."

About the Author

Rachel Nuwer is a science journalist and author. Her latest book is I Feel Love: MDMA and the Quest for Connection in a Fractured World *(Bloomsbury, 2023). Follow her on X @RachelNuwer.*

Why Dying People Often Experience a Burst of Lucidity

By Jordan Kinard

Long the fixation of religions, philosophy, and literature the world over, the conscious experience of dying has recently received increasingly significant attention from science. This comes as medical advances extend the ability to keep the body alive, steadily prying open a window into the ultimate locked room: the last living moments of a human mind.

"Around 1959 humans discovered a method to restart the heart in people who would have died, and we called this CPR," says Sam Parnia, a critical care physician at NYU Langone Health. Parnia has studied people's recollections after being revived from cardiac arrest—phenomena that he refers to as "recalled experiences surrounding death." Before CPR techniques were developed, cardiac arrest was basically synonymous with death. But now doctors can revive some people up to 20 minutes or more after their heart has stopped beating. Furthermore, Parnia says, many brain cells remain somewhat intact for hours to days postmortem—challenging our notions of a rigid boundary between life and death.

Advancements in medical technology and neuroscience, as well as shifts in researchers' perspectives, are revolutionizing our understanding of the dying process. Research over the past decade has demonstrated a surge in brain activity in human and animal subjects undergoing cardiac arrest. Meanwhile large surveys are documenting the seemingly inexplicable periods of lucidity that hospice workers and grieving families often report witnessing in people with dementia who are dying. Poet Dylan Thomas famously admonished his readers, "Do not go gentle into that good night. Rage, rage against the dying of the light." But as more resources are devoted to the study of death, it is becoming increasingly clear that dying is not the simple dimming of one's internal light of awareness but rather an incredibly active process in the brain.

What Is Terminal Lucidity?

For decades, researchers, hospice caregivers and stunned family members have watched with awe as people with Alzheimer's or other forms of dementia suddenly regain their memories and personalities just before death. To their family members it might seem like a second lease on life, but for many experienced medical workers, it can be a sign the end is near. Christopher Kerr, chief executive officer and chief medical officer at the Center for Hospice and Palliative Care in Buffalo, N.Y., has studied the lucid visions of several hundred terminally ill people. He says these events "usually occur in the last few days of life." Such "terminal lucidity" is defined as the unexpected return of cognitive faculties such as speech and "connectedness" with other people, according to George Mason University's Andrew Peterson, a researcher of bioethics and consciousness who co-authored a study of the phenomenon commissioned by the National Institutes of Health.

This connectedness goes beyond the return of lost communication ability and situational awareness. "One thing that seems to be quite profound for family members who observe lucidity is something we call the 'old self' emerging," Peterson says. "There seems to be clear evidence that they're aware not merely of their surroundings ... but additionally understanding what their relationships to other people are"—be it the use of a nickname or a reference to a longstanding inside joke.

As surprising as these events might seem, they are quite common. "Our study wasn't a prevalence study," says Jason Karlawish, a gerontologist at the Penn Memory Center and senior principal investigator of the NIH study. Nevertheless, he adds, "what we found is lucidity was more common than it was the exception in dementia patients, which would suggest that the idea of it being terminal is not entirely correct." Instead he suggests that episodes of lucidity should be seen as part of the "disease experience" rather than as aberrant events. "We've actually found that a variety of these episodes occurred months, even years, before the person died," Karlawish notes. Even so, many experts including Kerr and Parnia agree that most of these episodes are associated with the approach of death. "It's almost like they're preparing themselves to die," Parnia says.

The potential implications of these widespread, temporary cognitive resurgences are profound. "It suggests there may be neural networks that are remaining, and/or pathways and neural function, that could help potentially restore cognitive abilities to individuals we otherwise think are permanently impaired," Peterson says.

Nevertheless, research into this phenomenon is still in its early phases. "We don't actually know what's going on in the brain during the dying process that may in some way connect to these episodes," Peterson says. Despite this uncertainty, other research into brain activity near or at the time of death could provide scientists and clinicians greater insight into some of the processes occurring in the diseased and dying brain.

What Happens in the Brain as People Die?

In a study published in *Proceedings of the National Academy of Sciences USA* in May, researchers at the University of Michigan observed a surge of organized brain activity in two out of four comatose people who were undergoing cardiac arrest after being removed from life support. This work built on more than a decade of animal research, including a 2013 PNAS study that revealed a similar surge in synchronized brain activity in rats exposed to a cardiac toxin and a 2015 study in which rats were killed by asphyxiation. In all of these investigations, the researchers found that gamma-wave activity surged within the first few minutes of cardiac arrest and then ceased. Gamma waves are a frequency of brain wave typically associated with wakefulness, alertness, and memory recall.

Jimo Borjigin, a neurologist and an associate professor of molecular and integrative physiology at the University of Michigan, was involved in all three studies. The surge of gamma waves in dying subjects was particularly intense in a brain region Borjigin refers to as the "posterior cortical 'hot zone,'" located near the back of the skull. Some other researchers believe this region may also be essential to conscious experience. The parts of the brain in this area are related to visual, auditory and motion perception–a phenomenon Borjigin believes is involved in the out-of-body experiences reported by people who come close to death and recover. She adds that gamma-wave activation patterns akin to those observed in the comatose people are associated with activities that include the recognition of a familiar image–such as a human face–in healthy people.

In both the human and animal studies, the subjects' brain showed a spike in activity after the sudden reduction of oxygen supply, Borjigin says. "It starts to activate this homeostatic mechanism to get oxygen back, either by breathing harder or making your heart beat faster," she adds. Borjigin hypothesizes that much of the surge in more complex brain activity observed in humans and animals undergoing cardiac arrest is also a result of the brain attempting to reestablish homeostasis, or biological equilibrium, after detecting a lack of oxygen. She further speculates that these survival mechanisms may be involved in other changes in cognition surrounding death. "I believe dementia patients' terminal lucidity may be due to these kinds of last-ditch efforts of the brain" to preserve itself as physiological systems fail, Borjigin says.

NYU Langone's Parnia agrees that the brain's reaction to the loss of oxygen is at least partially responsible for lucid experiences surrounding death. Between 2017 and 2020 Parnia led a study called AWARE II, in which researchers monitored the brain activity of more than 500 critically ill people in the U.S. and U.K. who were receiving CPR. The patients were exposed to audiovisual stimuli while undergoing CPR to test their memory of events after cardiac arrest. Those who survived were later interviewed about how aware they were during the resuscitation process. According to Parnia, one in five survivors reported lucid experiences that occurred after their heart stopped. The AWARE II team also observed an unexpected spike in brain activity during CPR, he says. "Within 20 seconds of cardiac arrest, the brain flatlines," Parnia says. Yet "usually within five minutes–but it could be longer–we're seeing a reemergence of a transient period of brain electricity." He adds that the frequencies of brain activity observed are similar to those associated with conscious experience.

Parnia believes the dying brain loses the usual suppression mechanisms that allow us to focus on tasks during our day-to-day lives. "When you die, your brain is deprived of oxygen and nutrients, so it shuts down," Parnia says. "This shutting down process takes away the brakes ... and suddenly what seems to be happening is: it gives you access to parts of your brain that you normally can't access .... All your thoughts or your memories or your interactions with everyone else come out." But he stresses that the experiences of people undergoing cardiac arrest are lucid, not merely hallucinations. "They're not delusional," Parnia says of the resuscitated people he studied, and what they're experiencing is "not dreams or hallucinations." Although his previous studies focused on resuscitated critically ill people, Parnia believes that terminal lucidity in people who are comatose or have dementia may be the product of a similar process. He is currently participating in a study on the latter phenomenon.

A full explanation for the conscious experiences of dying people remains elusive. But research increasingly paints a picture of death as an incredibly active and complex process–and, perhaps more importantly, "a humanized one," as Kerr describes it. As for people with dementia, Karlawish says that rather than assuming their consciousness has been irrevocably changed, "we should still pay close attention to their mind because some aspects are still there, though they may be quite damaged."

About the Author

Jordan Kinard is a freelance writer in New York City. He has written about neuroscience, sustainability and other topics for Scientific American.

Thinking about Death Can Make Life Better

By Michael W. Wiederman

My father was just 32 years old when he was diagnosed with acute leukemia. Weeks later he was in the hospital, informed that he would not be leaving. Miraculously the leukemia went into remission, and he lived another five years. Even as a child, though, I could clearly see that the man who returned from the hospital was not the same one who had left home. Before, he had been concerned mostly with work and material success; now he embraced religion and family. Getting a second, tenuous chance at life was a profound experience that deeply changed his values and behavior.

We deflect it with humor, hedge against it with good works, shun reminders of our animal nature. Yet we all share the reality of mortality, and we know it, try as we might to throttle our thoughts about it. Indeed, this simultaneous knowing and recoiling from our knowledge is a tension that will run throughout our life. Yet despite the significance of the subject, for most of its history psychology has left the matter of how mortal thoughts affect us almost completely unexplored–terror incognita.

That neglect appears to be a thing of the past. In recent years researchers have begun to find that awareness of mortality affects our behavior in ways both overt and subtle and sometimes seems to pull us in opposite directions. Therapists who take an existential approach to counseling have found that confrontation with our mortality is worthwhile and beneficial. At the same time, a new discipline called terror management theory (TMT) has spawned hundreds of studies showing that awareness of our mortality can lead to selfish, even hurtful behavior.

More recently, this apparent disagreement among different disciplines, common enough in new fields of research, has given way to a deeper understanding of why our thoughts about mortality sometimes help us and sometimes do us harm. One essential determinant of how we handle the subject appears to be whether our life goals are material or idealistic. The effect of mortal thinking on behavior also seems to depend on whether death is at the top of our mind or hovering just beyond our consciousness. Still, the duality of helpful and harmful effects echoes one of life's central conundrums: we cannot deny that someday we will die, so how are we to keep this paralyzing truth from paralyzing us?

Facing Death Head-on

In one of my favorite cartoons, by Eric Lewis, a man lying on his deathbed says to his attentive wife, "I should have bought more crap." The dying man's regret is a tour de force of deflection and misdirection, the opposite of what we expect of a man looking back with rue. For most of us, a near-death experience or the death of someone we know prompts us to take stock of our life in a good way. This certainly was true for my father, and it is precisely the effect that existential therapists count on as they try to help their clients confront mortality and shift their life onto a more meaningful path. Typically the shift is from extrinsic values and goals, such as material success, toward intrinsic ones, such as matters of the soul or spirit.

Surveys validate the usefulness of the approach. In a study published in 2007 Emily L. B. Lykins, now at Eastern Kentucky University, and her colleagues questioned staff at a medical center in Northridge, Calif., two to three weeks after an earthquake in 1994 devastated the surrounding area, killing 57 and injuring thousands more. The staff were asked to rate the importance of 16 different goals both currently and as they were before the earthquake. The results indicated a shift in values toward intrinsic goals such as cultivating close relationships, doing creative work, and developing as a person. Moreover, those respondents who had most strongly feared they were going to die in the earthquake were also most likely to indicate a shift from extrinsic to intrinsic goals.

The beneficial effect works the other way around, too. People who pursue intrinsic goals have more success in heading off anxiety associated with death than those who chase material things. In 2009 Alain Van Hiel and Maarten Vansteenkiste of Ghent University in Belgium published their survey of older adults (with an average age of 75). The elders who reported having fulfilled more of their intrinsic goals were the least anxious about death and most satisfied with their life. In contrast, respondents who reported the greatest attainment of extrinsic goals indicated the most despair and the least acceptance of death.

Intrinsic life goals and the creation of meaning appear to be central to coping with our mortality. In 2012 William S. Breitbart and several colleagues at Memorial Sloan-Kettering Cancer Center in New York City published the results of an intervention with patients coping with advanced stages of cancer. The patients were randomly invited to participate in one of two groups that met once a week for eight weeks. The first group, which focused on social support, facilitated discussions about day-to-day concerns and ways to cope with them. The second group focused on the sources of meaning in life. At the end of the eight weeks and again at a two-month follow-up, members of the group focused on meaning in life showed substantial increases in their scores on measures of meaning, peace, and faith, along with decreases in anxiety and desire for death. The members of the group focused on social support showed no statistically significant changes.

Taming Terror

These surveys suggest that people who have an abrupt encounter with mortality tend to seek meaning in life, and those who pursue meaning in life can handle mortality more easily. People also seem to use systems of meaning to block awareness of their mortality, clinging to aspects of their life that provide connection with social structures.

How this protective shield might work is the focus of the burgeoning field of terror management theory. Based on the writings of cultural anthropologist Ernest Becker in the 1960s and 1970s and the more recent work of psychologists Jeff Greenberg of the University of Arizona, Tom Pyszczynski of the University of Colorado Colorado Springs and Sheldon Solomon of Skidmore College, TMT proposes that we humans maintain a shared culture because social roles and consequences for behavior keep us busy and so insulate us from the existential terror of our impermanence.

Interesting as such propositions are, they leave unanswered the question of whether our thoughts of mortality are what spur us to defend our culture and bolster our self-esteem or whether we just do what we do because it feels right. Psychologists needed a new approach to tease out how our mortal thoughts influence us.

Death in the Laboratory

Imagine you are staying with a friend who lives on the 20th floor of an old apartment building. It's the middle of the night. You are awakened from a deep sleep by the sound of screams and the choking smell of smoke. You run to the door and reach for the handle. You pull back in pain as the intense heat of the knob burns your skin. You grab a blanket from the bed for protection and manage to open the door. Almost immediately, a huge wall of flame and smoke roars into the room. It is getting very hard to breathe, and the heat from the flames is almost unbearable. You try calling out for help, but you can't find the air to form the words. With your heart pounding, it suddenly hits you that you are moments from dying. Out of breath and weak, you shut your eyes and wait for the end.

Fun thought exercise, yes? It is drawn from a 2003 study by Philip J. Cozzolino, now at the University of Essex in England, and his colleagues. Contemplating scenarios like it is how volunteers in some of the hundreds of TMT studies conducted during the past two decades were primed (and terrified) before they were put through their paces by researchers trying to see how reflection about death can affect human behavior.

Most TMT research focuses on the so-called mortality salience hypothesis: if investment in our culture and self-esteem serves to fend off our sense of mortality, then stimulating our awareness of mortality should increase investment in our culture and self-esteem. Researchers can arouse mortality salience in a variety of ways, but in most studies, participants are asked to write essays in which they imagine either death or some other kind of pain.

One group might be asked to visualize a scenario akin to the one above and to describe both what would happen to them physically as they died and the feelings kindled in them by thinking about their death. The control group might be asked to imagine and describe a less terminally uncomfortable event, such as an episode of dental pain or an experience of social exclusion. Then the researchers attempt to assess how the two groups differ in their self-esteem and their willingness to invest in their culture.

What researchers learned was that when thoughts of death reverberate too loudly, they can drown out subtle but important changes in our behavior. When we are made to concentrate on our mortality, we tend to defend against anxiety by direct means, primarily denial, rationalization, and a focus on the positive aspects of our life, boosting our sense of well-being by converting death into an abstraction that lies in the far future. Thus, if scientists measure investment in worldview or self-esteem immediately after increases in awareness of mortality (as with the group writing about death by fire), usually they see no apparent effects. The relations appear only when respondents are distracted after their awareness is heightened.

In a typical study, after completing the death essay (or the control essay), participants perform a filler task having nothing to do with death so that any unconscious defenses against mortality awareness have a chance to emerge. Only then comes a measurement of the participants' investment in their culture or self-esteem. Within this framework, researchers began to see that our mortality affects us in ways we do not even realize, especially in how it can transform our goals.

Religiosity and Creatureliness

Because religion is such an important aspect of our worldview (not least whether we are pro or con), it makes an especially useful starting point for researchers. Religious teachings tend to explain what happens to believers and nonbelievers after death, so defending one's religious beliefs in the face of mortality is particularly common. Yet a series of studies reported in 2006 by psychologists Ara Norenzayan of the University of British Columbia and Ian G. Hansen of York College showed that thoughts of death did more than make people with religious dispositions think of eternity at the right hand of God.

In the first of their studies, college students randomly assigned to write the standard death essay rated themselves about 30 percent higher on measures of religiosity and belief in God than did students assigned to write the control essay. What the experiment did not reveal was whether thoughts of death simply reminded people of their religious belief or prodded them to bolster their religiosity as a defense against mortality. To investigate this possibility, the second study randomly exposed college students to one of three versions of a brief story about a boy's visit to a hospital. All versions started and ended the same, but the middle passages differed. In the control version, the boy watched an emergency drill carried out by adults, in the religious version the boy observed a man praying in the hospital chapel, and in the death version the boy had an accident and died.

One of the distraction tasks in the experiment called for students to read a report of a study illustrating apparent effects of Christian prayer by strangers on the reproductive rates of women attending a fertility clinic. As part of their assessments of the study, participants were asked to rate their belief in God or in a higher power. The ratings by students in the control condition and religious condition did not differ, but both were significantly lower than the ratings by those in the death condition. It seems that mortality salience uniquely motivates people to bolster their religious beliefs.

Besides giving us a context for spirituality, culture also helps to protect us from thoughts of mortality through norms and customs that let us forget we are animals, which we know are mortal and die for capricious reasons. For example, elimination of bodily waste is taboo and performed in private, and our clothing and grooming typically help us avoid the smell and look of wild creatures. Our dining manners and rituals keep us from "eating like an animal," a charge that is clearly an insult.

TMT proposes that experiences that remind us of our animal nature will arouse awareness of our mortality, thus causing us to avoid them, especially if mortality salience is already heightened. How we might feel about seeing a woman breast-feeding her infant, for instance, seems to be influenced by whether we have been made aware of our mortality beforehand.

In 2007 Cathy Cox, now at Texas Christian University, and her colleagues published their research on this question. In their first study, college students rated their reaction to a written scenario in which a woman breast-feeds in a fancy restaurant, provoking a negative reaction from the restaurant staff. Volunteers who had been primed with the death essay rated the woman 40 percent more harshly than did the students primed by the dental pain essay.

Cox and her colleagues followed up by bringing breast-feeding into the lab, although no actual breast-feeding occurred. The researchers told college student participants that the study involved formation of impressions of another person before completing a task with that person. The subjects were advised that the other participant was a young woman who could not find child care and had to bring her infant along with her; she had arrived early and was feeding the child in the other room.

The students were randomly told either that the mother was breast-feeding or bottle-feeding and then were randomly assigned either to the standard death essay or to the dental pain essay. After filling out a questionnaire about hobbies and interests, the students were presented with what they believed was a like questionnaire that had been completed by the young mother in the other room. In reality, there was no such person, and all students were shown the same fictitious profile. They were then asked to rate their impressions of this other student with whom they would soon be working.

When rating the likability of this mystery woman, students who had written about dental pain returned similar ratings whether the woman was described as bottle-feeding or breast-feeding. Yet those primed with the death essay rated the young mother as less likable when she was said to be breast-feeding. Last, the participants were told it was time to perform the joint task with the young mother. They were taken to an empty room containing only two folding chairs leaning against the wall and were asked to set up the chairs, facing each other, in preparation for the task. The researchers were looking to see how closely the students placed the chairs. The distances between the two chairs were very similar in all but one condition: the students placed the chairs about 20 percent farther apart when they had been primed with the death essay and told that their partner had been breast-feeding.

It appears that when primed to think about our own mortality, we tend to disparage and distance ourselves from reminders that we humans are animals. Other researchers have demonstrated this phenomenon with people's reactions to the elderly, disabled individuals, and sexual activity. In an article published in 2000 the originators of TMT (Greenberg, Pyszczynski and Solomon) described research they conducted with their colleague Jamie Goldenberg, now at the University of South Florida. College students who underwent the standard method for inducing mortality salience rated the physical aspects of sex as less appealing compared with students who had not been so primed. The same researchers later found that students primed to focus on the romantic meaning of sex experienced fewer thoughts about death than did those primed to focus on the physical aspects of sex.

Handling Death

So what does all this tell us about how we might manage our fear of mortality? If brushes with death help people worry less about it and devote more energy to the things that give deeper meaning to life, then focused thinking about death might help the rest of us.

We already expose ourselves to death without knowing why. We watch slasher films, read violent novels and news accounts of tragic deaths, and share sick jokes about death and corpses. Such diversions might appeal to us because vicarious experiences of death can satisfy curiosity and address our anxiety in a way that keeps our own mortality at a safe remove. In fact, by choosing exposure to death we exert a degree of control. Death becomes something that prompts a laugh, a groan, or a thrill rather than terror. Culturally constructed scenarios of death may serve as a safety valve for venting anxiety.

Repeated exposure to death and dying in naturalistic settings also appears to lower discomfort around the topic. In 2008 Susan Bluck and her colleagues at the University of Florida published a study of hospice volunteers. Scores on a measure of death anxiety were lower for more experienced volunteers than for novices. Also, the best predictor of the level of their anxiety about death was not the length of time that the volunteers had served but the number of deaths that they had attended. Ironically, by prolonging human lives and removing our loved ones from their natural habitats when they are dying, medical technology has insulated us from experiences with death; greater anxiety about mortality may be a side effect.

One brief period of thinking about our mortality would probably do little good. Yet repeated contemplation of our eventual death could both lessen the anxiety about it and help keep us focused on the aspects of life that matter most.

Without such focused contemplation, thinking about the end of life is as likely to take us to the darkness as to the light. In a survey of nearly 1,000 students who took her Sociology of Death and Dying course at the University of Louisiana at Lafayette from 1985 to 2004, Sarah Brabant asked her students how often they thought about death. The most common responses were "occasionally" (58 percent) and "frequently" (20 percent). She also asked how the students felt when they thought of their own mortality. The two most common responses were "fearful" and "pleasure in being alive," each at 29 percent.

Within these few statistics lies the human condition. We cannot escape awareness of our mortality, and that awareness has the power to elicit fear or appreciation. Fortunately, the choice is ours.

Referenced

The Denial of Death. Ernest Becker. Free Press, 1973.

In the Wake of 9/11: The Psychology of Terror. T. Pyszczynski, S. Solomon and J. Greenberg. American Psychological Association, 2003.

"On the Unique Psychological Import of the Human Awareness of Mortality: Theme and Variations." T. Pyszczynski, J. Greenberg, S. Solomon and M. Maxfield in *Psychological Inquiry*, Vol. 17, No. 4, pages 328–355; 2006.

Staring at the Sun: Overcoming the Terror of Death. Irvin D. Yalom. Josey-Bass, 2008.

Flight from Death: The Quest for Immortality. Film directed by Patrick Shen. Transcendental Media, 2009. www.FlightFromDeath.com

"Death Anxiety and Its Role in Psychopathology: Reviewing the Status of a Transdiagnostic Construct." Lisa Iverach, Ross G. Menzies and Rachel E. Menzies in *Clinical Psychology Review*, Vol. 34, pages 580–593; 2014.

The Legal Definition of Death Needs to Be Clearer

By Ariane Lewis

As a neurologist who specializes in critical care, I believe we need a clearer, more consistent legal definition of death. The Uniform Determination of Death Act (UDDA), the legal standard for death throughout the U.S., has deficiencies, particularly with respect to the description of death by neurologic criteria, aka brain death. This causes confusion and moral distress for both families and health-care teams and can lead to protracted lawsuits about whether a person is alive or dead.

Historically, doctors declared death when a person was not breathing and had no heartbeat or palpable pulse. This occasionally caused controversy because they declared death prematurely. Declaring death became even more complicated as the 20th century progressed. Cardiopulmonary resuscitation (CPR) and ventilators allowed vital functions to continue in people who previously would have died. Some of these people were comatose as a result of catastrophic brain injuries and would never be able to breathe on their own because of damage to the lowest part of the brain stem.

In 1968 a group chaired by anesthesiologist Henry Beecher and composed of experts in neurology, physiology, biochemistry, law, and social ethics convened at Harvard University to examine the definition of "irreversible coma," which subsequently became known as "brain death/death by neurologic criteria." They noted that the characteristics of irreversible coma–a permanently nonfunctioning brain–included unreceptivity and unresponsiveness, no movements or spontaneous breathing (apnea), and no brain stem reflexes.

The group believed that this definition of death would not require statutory changes because the law treated the question of death as a matter to be determined by clinicians, whom, they felt, would accept these standards. But legal disputes prompted President Jimmy Carter and Congress to ask a commission to develop legal guidance on the definition of death. The commission collaborated with members of the American Bar Association, the American Medical Association, and the National Conference of Commissioners on Uniform State Laws, in addition to philosophers, religious officials, and ethicists. They produced the UDDA, a recommended statute, in 1981 with the goal that all states would adopt it. The UDDA indicates that death can be declared, in accordance with accepted medical standards, on one of two grounds: irreversible cessation of circulatory and respiratory functions or irreversible cessation of all functions of the entire brain, including the brain stem. Every state accepted the UDDA, in language or in spirit.

Over the past decade, however, highly publicized lawsuits and debates amongst clinicians, ethicists, philosophers and lawyers have shown weaknesses of the UDDA, which I believe we need to address. For example, the UDDA does not provide guidance about whether clinicians need to obtain consent from a person's family prior to a brain death evaluation or how to handle objections. Families sometimes ask clinicians not to perform a brain death evaluation or to continue ventilator support after a brain death declaration. They may refuse to accept that brain death is death according to their social, cultural, philosophical, or religious beliefs. This creates challenges for clinicians and hospitals because most states provide no legal guidance about whether to perform the evaluation and subsequently discontinue ventilator support after a declaration of brain death in spite of objections or to provide families the ability to opt out. California and New York State vaguely require reasonable accommodation of objections, and Illinois notes that religious beliefs should be taken into consideration when determining time of death. New Jersey law uniquely states that if a patient is known to have religious beliefs that oppose a declaration of brain death, ventilator support and all other medical interventions should be continued until their heart stops beating. All this variation adds confusion. We need a consistent national approach to the declaration of death.

Additionally, some experts—such as Michael Nair-Collins, an associate professor of behavioral sciences and social medicine at Florida State University College of Medicine—argue that the medical brain death guidelines do not fit the UDDA's requirement for "irreversible cessation of all functions of the entire brain, including the brainstem." Nair-Collins believes that to be in accordance with the UDDA, the brain death evaluation should require assessment for loss of hormonal secretion from the pituitary gland and hypothalamus. No country requires this, however.

In 2021 the Uniform Law Commission (ULC) convened a drafting committee to discuss revisions to the UDDA. The purpose of the ULC is to strengthen the federal system by generating consistent rules across states. The commissioners invited participation from more than 100 people with relevant expertise, including representatives from medical, organ procurement, and advocacy organizations. Unfortunately, although there was widespread support for revising the UDDA, in the fall of 2023 the commission paused the drafting committee's work indefinitely because of concerns that diverse views about death would prevent the revisions from being widely adopted.

Like most of my medical colleagues who sent comments to the ULC, I favor changing the UDDA to align the law with clinical practice. For example, instead of the controversial phrase "cessation of all functions of the entire brain, including the brainstem," the law should state that brain death declaration requires coma, loss of brain stem reflexes, and inability to breathe spontaneously in the setting of an adequate stimulus.

There will always be varying religious, philosophical, ethical, and cultural perspectives on death, but society needs a clear legal standard that is consistent with medical practice throughout the country. Given that the ULC was not able to accomplish this, I believe this may need to be addressed on a national level.

The views expressed in this article are those of the author and do not represent any affiliated organization.

This is an opinion and analysis article, and the views expressed by the author or authors are not necessarily those of Scientific American.

About the Author

Ariane Lewis is a professor of neurology and neurosurgery and director of neurocritical care at NYU Langone Medical Center. She is also a fellow of both the Neurocritical Care Society and the American Academy of Neurology.

Section 3: Mass Death

There Is Nothing Normal about 1 Million People Dead from COVID

By Steven W. Thrasher

Despite being the wealthiest nation on the planet, the U.S. has continued to have by far the most COVID infections and deaths per country: one million dead, with no end in sight. This is an unfathomable number, yet in contrast to the beginning of the pandemic, the news media has often downplayed the 1 million mark. In May 2020 the *New York Times* ran a sympathetic headline reading "U.S. Deaths Near 100,000, an Incalculable Loss," using its entire front page to print names of some of the deceased. But when the death toll reached nine times that number, the *Times* callously wrote, "900,000 Dead, but Many Americans Move On."

The *Times* wasn't alone; several large mainstream publications, as well as politicians of both major political parties, have been beating a drum to get "back to normal" for months. The effect has been the manufactured consent to normalize mass death and suffering–to subtly suggest to Americans that they want to move on.

The media has helped to shape public opinion so business can return to the very circumstances that created this ongoing crisis. A return to normal would allow companies to reap profits, while some people work in relative safety from their homes (the target audience of many news organizations' advertisers) at the expense of more vulnerable people who must work or study in person.

This past winter David Leonhardt, the writer of the *Times*'s newsletter "The Morning," asked Michael Barbaro, the host of the company's podcast "The Daily": "If COVID is starting to look like a regular respiratory virus, is it rational for us to treat it like something completely different and to disrupt our lives in all these big and consequential ways[?]"

About 200,000 children in the U.S. have lost one or both parents because of COVID–roughly one in every 375 children. This is a big and consequential loss, and those children are probably not among the many who are ready to "move on." So is it rational? To be calling for the end of lifesaving mitigation efforts and saying they harm children when so many have been orphaned here and worldwide?

Is it rational for Democrats, Republicans, and much of the news media to press on toward what writer Tom Scocca calls a policy of "unlimited" COVID?

Is it rational, when as many people have died of COVID in a month as died of AIDS in its worst year (near 50,000 in 1995), to think of the novel coronavirus as a "regular respiratory virus"–and to think that the big and consequential disruptions to worry about are mask wearing and ventilation and not death and debilitation?

Is it rational to ignore high community viral loads in American society and to not do more to lower them so that fewer people are exposed, become sick, transmit onward and possibly die?

Well, it depends on what it is you are trying to rationalize.

If you're trying to get people to accept that what the nation has been doing is OK and that 50,000 deaths in a month should be normalized, then it's rational.

If you don't want people to wonder why in just two years the U.S. death toll for COVID was about 130 percent of the death toll of four decades of HIV–while global COVID deaths amount to less than 20 percent of the world's AIDS deaths–then it's rational.

If you want to manufacture consent for looser pandemic measures in the U.S. rather than more comprehensive ones as communal viral rates demand, then making these claims is rational.

But it's not ethical to manufacture what I call a viral underclass, and it's incorrect to pretend the news media have no role in creating it or in persuading the public that so many deaths are inevitable.

It's a shame that major news outlets are hyping up moving on and returning to normal and not running more pieces calling for an increase in government-funded mitigation efforts (more free high-quality masks and tests, upgraded ventilation in work sites and schools) to stem the tide of death. American norms (rampant incarceration, eviction, homelessness, lack of health care, poor ventilation, and economic inequality) are fairly deadly as is.

Acceding to the "urgency of normal" is "wishful thinking," epidemiologist Gregg Gonsalves wrote in the *Nation*. Intentionally or unintentionally, "the urgency of normal"—a phrase cropping up a lot lately—is evocative of a phrase Martin Luther King, Jr., used in his 1967 speech "Beyond Vietnam" at Riverside Church in New York City, where he preached about "the fierce urgency of now": "We are now faced with the fact that tomorrow is today. We are confronted with the fierce urgency of now. In this unfolding conundrum of life and history there is such a thing as being too late. Procrastination is still the thief of time."

If he were still alive, do you think King would have fought for the fierce urgency of the very normal that produced all this death?

About the Author

Steven W. Thrasher is a professor at Northwestern University in the Medill School of Journalism and the Institute for Sexual and Gender Minority Health and Wellbeing. He is author of the forthcoming book The Viral Underclass: The Human Toll When Inequality and Disease Collide. *Follow Thrasher on X (formerly Twitter) @thrasherxy.*

Death by Primordial Black Hole

By Avi Loeb

In the infant universe, a substantial enhancement in the radiation density on the scale of the cosmic horizon could have made some small regions behave as a closed universe and sealed their fate in isolated collapses to black holes.

The typical variations that are actually observed in the cosmic microwave background radiation had an initial amplitude that is 100,000 times smaller than needed to make black holes. But these variations can only be observed on large spatial scales. It is possible that rare density enhancements of a much larger amplitude were generated on very small scales as a result of new physics at high energies. Although existing cosmological data just allows for that, there is added motivation to consider this hypothetical possibility because of the existence of dark matter.

Most of the matter in the universe is dark, and despite searches for signatures of related elementary particles on the sky or in laboratory experiments, none were found so far. Primordial black holes (PBHs) could potentially make the dark matter. Various astrophysical constraints rule out PBHs as the dark matter if they have either low or high masses, but allow for a range of masses between a billionth and a thousandth of the mass of the moon–similar to asteroids with a size ranging between one and a hundred miles.

Sixty-six million years ago, an asteroid in this size range impacted Earth and killed the dinosaurs as well as three quarters of all life forms. This is a sober reminder that even the sky is a source of risks. We could protect ourselves from future asteroid impacts by searching for reflected sunlight from their surfaces upon their approach to Earth. In 2005, the U.S. Congress tasked NASA to find 90 percent of all hazardous objects larger than 140 meters, about a hundred times below the size of the Chicxulub impactor that killed the dinosaurs.

This led to the construction of survey telescopes like Pan STARRS and the forthcoming Vera C. Rubin Observatory, which can fulfil two thirds of the congressional goal. These surveys take advantage of the sun as a lamppost that illuminates the dark space near us. An early alert would allow us to deflect dangerous asteroids away from Earth. But PBHs do not reflect sunlight and cannot be identified this way ahead of impact. They do glow faintly in Hawking radiation, but their luminosity is lower than a mini light bulb of 0.1 watt for masses above a millionth of the mass of the moon. Is this invisibility a reason for concern?

In particular, if PBHs in the allowed mass range make up the dark matter, one may wonder whether they pose a threat to our life. An encounter of a PBH with a human body would represent a collision of an invisible relic from the first femtosecond after the big bang with an intelligent body–a pinnacle of complex chemistry made 13.8 billion years later. Although this constitutes a meeting of an extraordinary kind between the early and late universe, we would not wish it upon ourselves.

Let me explain.

To illustrate, I will focus on the upper end of the allowed mass window, at which the dark matter is made of PBHs with a thousandth of the mass of the moon. Smaller PBHs could be more common, but their effect is weaker. The horizon size of such a PBH is merely 1,000 times larger than the size of an atom.

One would naively expect that such a small object passing through our body would only result in a minor injury confined to a limited cylindrical trail of microscopic width. This would be the case for an energetic particle, like a cosmic ray, passing like a miniature projectile through our body. But this expectation ignores the long-range influence of gravity. The attractive gravitational force induced by a PBH of the abovementioned mass would shrink our entire body by several inches during its quick passage. The pull would be impulsive, lasting 10 microseconds for the typical PBH speed of 100 miles per second in the dark matter halo of the Milky Way galaxy. The resulting pain would feel as if a tiny vacuum cleaner with a tremendous suction power went quickly through our body and shrunk its muscles, bones, blood vessels and internal organs.

The dramatic bodily distortion would create severe damage and cause immediate death. How likely is it for us to experience a fatal event of this type during our life?

Gladly, a back-of-the-envelope estimate relieves all worries. If PBHs of the above mass make the dark matter, the chance of a PBH passing through our body during our entire lifetime is miniscule, only one part in 10^{26}. This translates to a small probability of order 10^{-16} for a single death in the entire population of 8 billion people living on Earth at present. The likelihood of one death increases to 10^{-9} if the current population size persists for another billion years, after which the expanding sun is expected to boil off all oceans on Earth. And if we assume similar statistics concerning stars within other galaxies, then only up to a trillion people in the entire observable volume of the universe might be killed by the passage of PBHs through their bodies. It is extremely safe to assume that any of us will not be one of these people. The total number of deaths might be larger in the multiverse if it contains many more volumes with similar conditions, and if even more dangerous types of dark matter exist in parts of it.

Nevertheless, it is possible that rare, invisible objects in the outskirts of the solar system, like the hypothesized Planet Nine, are PBHs. In a recent paper that I wrote with my student Amir Siraj, we showed that PBHs could be detected with the Vera C. Rubin Observatory throughout the entire solar system by the flares they generate when they encounter rocks from the Oort cloud.

Obviously, the risks for life on Earth from other catastrophes like asteroid impacts are far greater as the dinosaurs learned from firsthand experience. The above numbers imply that we should not lose sleep or upgrade our medical insurance coverage over concerns about invisible PBHs that may be lurking in the Milky Way's halo. During these days of looming risks from pandemics and climate change, this is a refreshingly positive message from Mother Nature that we should happily embrace.

This is an opinion and analysis article.

About the Author

Avi Loeb is former chair (2011-2020) of the astronomy department at Harvard University, founding director of Harvard's Black Hole Initiative and director of the Institute for Theory and Computation at the Harvard-Smithsonian Center for Astrophysics. He also chairs the Board on Physics and Astronomy of the National Academies and the advisory board for the Breakthrough Starshot project, and is a member of President's Council of Advisors on Science and Technology. Loeb is the bestselling author of Extraterrestrial: The First Sign of Intelligent Life Beyond Earth *(Houghton Mifflin Harcourt).*

The U.S. Just Lost 26 Years' Worth of Progress on Life Expectancy

By Tanya Lewis

With a few notable exceptions—such as during the 1918 influenza pandemic, World War II, and the HIV crisis—life expectancy in the U.S. has had a gradual upward trajectory over the past century. But that progress has steeply reversed in the past two years as COVID and other tragedies have cut millions of lives short.

U.S. life expectancy fell by a total of 2.7 years between 2019 and 2021 to 76.1 years—the lowest it has been since 1996, according to provisional data recently released by the Centers for Disease Control and Prevention's National Center for Health Statistics (NCHS). The drop was 3.1 years for male individuals and 2.3 years for female ones. Non-Hispanic Native American and Alaska Native peoples saw the biggest decline—a staggering 6.6 years. But every racial and ethnic group suffered: life expectancy decreased by 4.2 years in the Hispanic population, by four years in the non-Hispanic Black population, by 2.4 years in the non-Hispanic white population and by 2.1 years in the non-Hispanic Asian population.

"Basically, all the gains between 1996 and 2019 are as if they never happened," says Elizabeth Arias, director of the U.S. life table program at the NCHS and co-author of a report on the new data.

COVID deaths drove much of the decline as the country grappled with the world's worst pandemic in a century. But unintentional injuries—largely driven by drug overdoses—also played a significant role, the data show. Increases in deaths from heart disease, chronic liver disease, and suicide also contributed.

"This isn't supposed to happen," says Philip Cohen, a professor of sociology at the University of Maryland, who studies demographic trends and inequality. "I think it's a wake-up call for us ... that we can't put public health on autopilot; that we don't have this invisible hand of development just raising living standards over time."

The drop in life expectancy would have been even more stark if it had not been partially offset by declines in influenza and pneumonia deaths, which were likely reduced by pandemic-related precautions such as masking and social distancing.

Arias and her colleagues calculated life expectancy using a technique called a period life table. This involved the researchers imagining a group of 100,000 hypothetical infants and applying the death rates observed for the real population in 2021 for each year of those infants' lives. The result is not the life expectancy for a cohort of actual babies born in 2021 but rather a snapshot of how life expectancy rates would apply to various age groups at a specific point in time, Arias says.

The data show that in 2021 the Native American and Alaska Native populations had the lowest life expectancy of any race or ethnicity: 65.2 years. This is equivalent to the life expectancy of the total U.S. population in 1944, Arias and her colleagues wrote. Indigenous peoples, who already had high rates of chronic disease and poor health care access before the pandemic, were disproportionately impacted by COVID.

These outcomes have their roots in colonialist U.S. government policies, says Crystal Lee, an assistant professor at the University of New Mexico's College of Population Health and CEO of the nonprofit organization United Natives, as well as a health services company called Indigenous Health. "There have just been so many policies that have been harmful to Native Americans throughout all these years," says Lee, who is Diné and from the Navajo Nation. Native American tribes are officially recognized as sovereign. But they are also still designated as "domestic dependent nations," meaning they are subject to the U.S. federal government. The government provides funding for education, housing, and health care–the latter through the Indian Health Service–but all of these have long been underfunded, according to Lee. "We don't have the resources or the infrastructure or even adequate medical staffing," she says.

When the pandemic hit, Lee and her nonprofit organization helped distribute supplies such as masks and cleaning products to the Navajo Nation and the Apache Nations, she says. She also started Indigenous Health to help provide quarantine housing for Native American people exposed to COVID. Many of them had overcrowded housing–or no housing at all–to go back to, and some were struggling with addiction, she says.

The second-biggest contributor to the life expectancy decline of the total U.S. population was unintentional injuries, of which a large fraction were opioid and other drug overdoses. Such deaths, as well as those related to alcohol and suicide–sometimes called "deaths of despair"–have spiked in the years leading up to and during the pandemic. Drug overdose deaths reached more than 100,000 annually during the 12 months ending in April 2021. Opioid overdoses were initially concentrated among the white population, but they have now become more common in the Indigenous, Hispanic, and Black populations as well.

Cohen says COVID may have exacerbated the opioid crisis because people who lost family members and jobs turned to drugs and may have been less able to access treatment. "One crisis doesn't wait for another" to finish, he says.

Native American and Alaska Native individuals, along with Hispanic and Black people, suffered disproportionately high death rates during the pandemic's first year because many worked in essential jobs with a high COVID exposure risk. But the group with the second-largest drop in life expectancy from 2020 to 2021 was the non-Hispanic white population. Almost half of the total loss of life expectancy of the white population occurred in the pandemic's second year, Arias says. Lower vaccination rates and more resistance to masking and other precautions among the U.S.'s white population (compared with other races or ethnicities) is one possible explanation. White Americans are more likely to have voted for Donald Trump, and areas that voted for Trump have had higher rates of COVID deaths since the fall of 2020. Additionally, COVID took longer to reach rural parts of the country, which are more likely to have a largely white population.

The gender gap in life expectancy also widened. Historically, women have lived longer than men across every race and ethnicity. The gap between male and female life expectancy had been narrowing in the past decade, however. Women were living 4.8 years longer than men in 2010, but the pandemic erased some of that narrowing, and the gap widened to 5.9 years in 2021. Men are more likely than women to die of COVID, studies have shown. In addition, unintentional injury deaths (largely overdoses)–which have increased–are more common among men.

Despite being the richest country in the world, the U.S. has one of the lowest life expectancies of any developed country. And it has seen one of the largest declines in life expectancy among such countries during the pandemic, according to World Bank data. Part of this likely stems from a high rate of socioeconomic inequality.

"One of the things that affected me the most–even though I'm used to seeing these numbers ... was the fact that there's such large disparities in life expectancy in the U.S.," Arias says. The Native American population has a life expectancy comparable to that of some of poorest countries in Africa, she notes. "It's kind of amazing, when you sit back and think about it, that we have in this country a population that has the same life expectancy as a really poor developing country."

Addressing these gaps in life expectancy would require the U.S. to overhaul its health care system and make it work for everyone, many experts say. For Native Americans in particular, that means public awareness, allyship. and accountability. "We need to hold the U.S. government accountable by honoring the existent treaties," Lee says. She believes there also needs to be more awareness about Native American people, who she says have become invisible. People need to know, she says, "that we're still here in the United States, and we're still existent."

About the Author

Tanya Lewis is a senior editor covering health and medicine at Scientific American. *She writes and edits stories for the website and print magazine on topics ranging from COVID to organ transplants. She also appears on* Scientific American's *podcast Science, Quickly and writes* Scientific American's *weekly Health & Biology newsletter. She has held a number of positions over her seven years at* Scientific American, *including health editor, assistant news editor and associate editor at* Scientific American Mind. *Previously, she has written for outlets that include* Insider, Wired, Science News, *and others. She has a degree in biomedical engineering from Brown University and one in science communication from the University of California, Santa Cruz. Follow her on X @tanyalewis314 and Bluesky @tanyalewis.bsky.social.*

Section 4: Preventing Death

A Common Antibiotic Could Prevent Deaths from Childbirth Complications

By Allison Parshall

Childbirth is a vulnerable experience, both emotionally and physically. Giving birth, whether vaginally or through a cesarean section, creates opportunities for bacteria to infect both the parent and newborn, and sometimes these infections can cause the parent's immune response to spiral out of control.

That extreme response to infection, called sepsis, is the third most common global cause of death during or after childbirth. Millions of cases of maternal sepsis occur each year, mostly in low- and middle-income countries. It can be particularly difficult for doctors to detect and treat it in time because the usual symptoms of sepsis–such as fever, fast heart rate, and low blood pressure–can also be present during a healthy pregnancy and childbirth. If left untreated, sepsis can cause tissue damage, organ failure, and ultimately death.

To prevent these infections during a cesarean section, doctors routinely administer an antibiotic called azithromycin before beginning surgery. Now a global study in low- and middle-income countries shows that the same approach may prevent sepsis in vaginal deliveries too. In settings with limited health-care resources, giving people planning to give birth vaginally a single dose of azithromycin lowered their risk of sepsis by 35 percent. Because azithromycin is inexpensive and can be taken orally, this approach may be a feasible way to prevent some cases of maternal sepsis in countries with limited health-care access, where sepsis during or after childbirth is more common. The results were published in the *New England Journal of Medicine.*

The study is "such an incredibly exciting story because it adds to our ability to take better care of these women and ultimately to hopefully change their outcomes," says Laura Riley, an ob-gyn at Weill Cornell Medicine in New York City, who was not involved in the research.

The study followed nearly 30,000 participants from seven countries: Bangladesh, India, Pakistan, Zambia, Kenya, the Democratic Republic of the Congo, and Guatemala. The researchers followed the participants for more than a month after they gave birth. Of the participants who received the antibiotic, 1.6 percent experienced sepsis, compared with 2.5 percent of those who did not receive the treatment. This was a larger decrease than the study's architects had anticipated, and the participants experienced minimal side effects. The antibiotic did not impact the rate of newborn infections or deaths.

"We were excited," says Alan Tita, an ob-gyn at the University of Alabama at Birmingham and the study's lead author. "It's just awesome because of the potential to make a huge difference in the care and outcomes for patients." The research team had planned to enroll more participants, but the early results were conclusive enough to end the study early.

"It's a wonderfully pleasant surprise to see an effect that large," says Michael Santos of the Foundation for the National Institutes of Health, one of the funding partners of the study. "That's a really spectacular result."

If a person survives sepsis, it can cause lifelong damage. "You can lose fingers and toes and do damage to internal organs like your kidneys and your liver and your brain," Riley says.

Fortunately, sepsis is often preventable. "I do think that the study alone may be enough to change practice," says Lindsay Admon, an ob-gyn studying health equity at the University of Michigan, who was not involved in the study. The rate of maternal mortality in the United States has been increasing since the late 1990s and is more than twice as high as it is in other wealthy nations. Here the racial inequality is stark, with Black people being nearly three times more likely to die from childbirth than white people, according to the Centers for Disease Control and Prevention. Admon would like to see a similar study done in the U.S. and other high-income countries that nonetheless have large health disparities.

The benefit of prescribing azithromycin for sepsis prevention needs to be weighed against the consequences of overusing antibiotics, however. These drugs save lives, but in the process, they pressure bacteria to find a way to evade them. Drug-resistant bacteria are on the rise, and they can be deadly. Azithromycin in particular targets a wide range of bacteria, which is why it works well in childbirth. Yet this amplifies its risk of leaving drug-resistant microbes behind. This trade-off is crucial to weighing the benefit of this intervention, says Mercedes Bonet Semenas, a medical officer at the World Health Organization's Department of Sexual and Reproductive Health and Research, who wasn't involved in the new paper.

"That question is on everyone's mind and was part of the study design," Santos says. The researchers are continuing to analyze samples taken from participants to determine the drug's precise effects on the naturally occurring bacteria in their patients' body. They expect those results to be published in 2024.

Preventing sepsis may be worth the risk of contributing to antibiotic resistance in areas of the world where infections during childbirth are common. "The study is the first step," says Julie Gerberding, CEO of the Foundation for the National Institutes of Health. Getting the medication to those who can use it most will require a coordinated global effort. The WHO could review the results and choose to include the treatment in its essential medicines program, as well as its guidelines for obstetric care, Gerberding says.

Maternal mortality is a "conspicuous area of inequality," she says. "Now this is a chance to tackle a very, very dangerous dimension of birth."

About the Author

Allison Parshall is an associate news editor at Scientific American *who often covers biology, health, technology and physics. She edits the magazine's Contributors column and weekly online Science Quizzes. As a multimedia journalist, Parshall contributes to* Scientific American's *podcast Science Quickly. Her work includes a three-part miniseries on music-making artificial intelligence. Her work has also appeared in* Quanta Magazine *and* Inverse. *Parshall graduated from New York University's Arthur L. Carter Journalism Institute with a master's degree in science, health and environmental reporting. She has a bachelor's degree in psychology from Georgetown University. Follow Parshall on X (formerly Twitter) @parshallison.*

ECPR Could Prevent Many More Cardiac Arrest Deaths

By Erica Westly

Every year more than 300,000 people in the U.S. die from an out-of-hospital cardiac arrest, making it a leading cause of death. Improved access to cardiopulmonary resuscitation (CPR) and defibrillators–devices that use an electric shock to restore a person's heartbeat–have helped increase survival rates somewhat, but about 90 percent of cases are still fatal. Recent studies have found that combining traditional CPR with a process called extracorporeal membrane oxygenation (ECMO), which helps deliver oxygen to the brain and other vital organs via a device similar to a heart-lung bypass machine, can significantly boost a person's chances of survival after cardiac arrest.

In 2020 a randomized clinical trial of this approach, known as extracorporeal cardiopulmonary resuscitation (ECPR), at the University of Minnesota showed that the technique resulted in a survival rate of 43 percent, compared with 7 percent in standard care. The result was deemed so successful that the National Institutes of Health terminated the study early, arguing that it would be unethical to deprive eligible people of the treatment.

The Minnesota trial focused on a subset of cardiac arrests that initially responded to defibrillation, but other studies indicate that ECPR can help in nonshockable cases, too. Still, technical and logistical challenges may keep the procedure from becoming the standard of care for cardiac arrest outside of large academic hospitals.

The basic technology behind ECPR has existed since the 1950s, when both CPR and the first heart-lung machines were developed. Although the ECMO process, during which a person's blood is removed, oxygenated, and pumped back into their body, became simpler over time, it was mostly used in operating rooms and neonatal intensive care units. That changed in 2009 when physicians in Asia began using ECMO to treat people who were hospitalized with H1N1 influenza, and the technology became more widely available. Use of ECMO during the COVID pandemic further increased interest in the approach.

But treating cardiac arrest with ECMO can be expensive—costing hospitals tens of thousands of dollars per patient—and technically challenging. The ECPR team at the University of Minnesota is considered one of the best in the world. Demetri Yannopoulos, director of the university's resuscitation medicine center, is a highly trained and experienced specialist, and the university's hospital is fully equipped to handle ECPR patients and provide them with the lengthy and involved care they frequently require after the procedure. "If you don't give people time to survive, you are going to have worse outcomes," Yannopoulos says.

Other hospitals have failed to find a clear benefit from ECPR. A study published earlier this year by a group in the Netherlands found no significant difference in survival rates between people who received ECPR after a cardiac arrest and those who didn't. None of the hospitals involved in the study had much experience administering ECPR, however, and it took them considerably longer, on average, than the University of Minnesota hospital to complete the procedure successfully—a crucial factor, given the time-sensitive nature of cardiac arrest.

One of the main reasons cardiac arrest is so deadly is that it occurs rapidly. Unlike a heart attack, which can develop gradually over hours, cardiac arrest typically occurs suddenly and without warning. Within seconds, the heart stops beating, and blood stops circulating, cutting off the brain's oxygen supply. Chest compressions can restore blood circulation but only partially. "CPR is not perfect. It circulates blood far less effectively than regular circulation," says Joseph Tonna, an emergency intensivist who performs ECPR at the University of Utah.

In contrast, ECPR can fully restore a person's circulation. It's also invasive and more complicated to execute, however. A clinician—usually a physician with specialized training—has to insert large tubes into a patient's femoral blood vessels while that person receives chest compressions. The procedure can also cause excess bleeding because people are often given blood thinners to prevent clots, which can clog the ECMO device that oxygenates the blood. All the while, the clock is ticking, with the likelihood of survival dropping by about 20 percent every 10 minutes.

For many people who have a cardiac arrest, ECPR is not even an option because they live too far away from a large hospital, where, until recently, ECPR had to be performed. Experts have been working to change that, though. Yannopoulos's team in Minneapolis has started using an ECMO-equipped vehicle to reach people in rural and suburban areas, as have groups in a few other cities. In 2019 a team at the University of New Mexico debuted an ambulance outfitted with a hand-crank-powered ECMO machine, which makes the device easier to set up and more affordable to use. "I'm really trying to get it as simple as possible," says Jonathan Marinaro, an emergency medicine professor at the university, who spearheaded the program.

Eventually, perhaps in the next 10 years, Tonna says, the ECPR process may become simple enough that nonphysicians will be able to perform it, which could greatly expand the procedure's use. But increasing the number of hospitals that currently offer ECPR could also potentially save many lives because enough of the roughly 350,000 out-of-hospital cardiac arrests that occur in the U.S. per year happen near health-care facilities. A recent study calculated that fewer than 2 percent of people in the U.S. who have a cardiac arrest are eligible for ECPR, based on their location and patient selection criteria. "The challenge is the variability in our health care system," says Cindy Hsu, an emergency physician and intensivist at the University of Michigan, who co-authored the study.

Even hospitals that have an ECMO program may not be prepared to care for people who've had a cardiac arrest after they've received ECPR. Complications, including internal bleeding and multiple organ failure, may necessitate surgery and other interventions. Additionally, people have to be treated for the underlying problems that led to their cardiac arrest. Clinicians want to ensure that people get adequate time to recover. There are also concerns, however, that ECPR could leave people in an untenable state if, for example, they survive but are left with severe brain damage or are unable to survive outside the hospital. "That is absolutely a problem with ECMO, but it's a problem with every new technology that offers life support," says Stephen Latham, director of the Yale University Interdisciplinary Center for Bioethics.

Ultimately, ECPR is not a cure for cardiac arrest. "It's basically a salvage intervention–perfusing and giving the body time to recover, if it can," Yannopoulos says. Yet for now, it may be the best chance of survival for people whose life would otherwise be cut short. "Some of these patients are quite young, so we're extending their lives by another several decades, and they can have a functional life afterward," Hsu says.

About the Author

Erica Westly is an author and journalist based in Seattle. Her work has appeared in Scientific American, Nature Medicine *and the* New York Times, *among other outlets.*

Ways to Extend Your Healthy Years, Not Just Your Life

By Lydia Denworth

Over the past century the average life expectancy in developed countries has increased by 30 years, from roughly age 50 to 80. Vaccines, sanitation, antibiotics, and other advances allow many more people to survive infectious diseases that used to kill them during childhood. (In the U.S., though, the span dropped by nearly three years during the COVID pandemic, a testament to the power of infections to shorten lives.)

Longer lifespans overall have been a public health success. But they have also created a new and important gap: healthspans, usually defined as the period of life free of chronic disease or disability, do not always match longevity. In this, my 12th year of caring for a relative with Alzheimer's disease, I know this fact well.

By one calculation, based on the World Health Organization's healthy life expectancy indicator, an American who expects to live to 79 might first face serious disease at 63. That could mean 15 years (20 percent of life) lived in sickness. Indeed, aging is the biggest risk factor for cancer, heart disease, and dementia.

One reason for this gap is that, for decades, biomedical research and clinical practice have focused on treating individual diseases, which can extend lives but not necessarily healthspan.

During the past 10 years medicine has started to take a different approach based on the biology of aging (a field called geroscience). "We're now saying our focus should be on extending healthy life rather than just length of life, and slowing aging is the tool to do it," says Jay Olshansky, a longevity expert at the University of Illinois at Chicago. There are molecular and cellular processes in all our tissues and organs that determine both lifespan and healthspan. These "pillars of aging" include DNA damage, the aging or senescence of individual cells, inflammation, and stress responses.

Natural variations in these factors are mostly the result of environmental differences. Genes also play a role, accounting for about 25 percent of the variability, more in extreme cases. (Very long-lived smokers probably won the genetic lottery.) The upshot is that some people age faster than others, and with biological aging comes susceptibility to disease and disability.

How do you assess biological age? Molecular markers such as chemical modifications to DNA are one way, says computational biologist Morgan Levine of Altos Labs in San Diego. "Do your cells have a pattern of chemical tags like someone who is 20 or 30 or 40?" she asks.

Geroscientists have yet to deliver a pill or treatment that can slow or reverse what the pillars of aging do. But they are excited about some possibilities. For example, senolytic drugs target senescent cells, which no longer divide but linger in the body instead of being cleared by the immune system. Research has shown that these "zombie cells" secrete proteins that interfere with other cells' health. The zombies have been linked to osteoarthritis, cancer, and dementia. For a 2015 study, researchers used senolytics to remove senescent cells in mice and delayed, prevented, or alleviated multiple disorders. Clinical trials are underway in people but are years from completion, so researchers are cautious. They also note that few popular wellness claims about "prolonging your youth" are grounded in evidence.

For now, one way to extend healthspan is through unsurprising preventive maintenance. Experts recommend checkups, staying on top of cholesterol levels and blood pressure, and following guidelines such as those from the *American Journal of Clinical Nutrition* for body fat percentage, lean body mass, and bone density. "Know where you are so if something needs to be tweaked you can take steps to do that," says Matt Kaeberlein, founding director of the University of Washington Healthy Aging and Longevity Research Institute and now chief executive officer of Optispan, a health tech company.

Those steps are also familiar: common-sense nutrition, sleep, exercise, and social connection are the four main factors. "The reason those things work is because they modulate the biology of aging," Kaeberlein says. For example, regular low- or moderate-intensity exercise helps to prevent cardiovascular disease and type 2 diabetes. How much extra health can these steps get us? "Ten years is probably pretty realistic," Kaeberlein says.

About the Author

Lydia Denworth is an award-winning science journalist and contributing editor for Scientific American. *She is author of* Friendship *(W. W. Norton, 2020).*

Eat (Less) to Live (Longer)

By Nikhil Swaminathan

Scientists have known for more than 70 years that the one surefire way to extend the lives of animals was to cut calories by an average of 30 to 40 percent. The question was: Why?

Now a new study begins to unravel the mystery and the mechanism by which reducing food intake protects cells against aging and age-related diseases.

Researchers report in the journal *Cell* that the phenomenon is likely linked to two enzymes–SIRT3 and SIRT4–in mitochondria (the cell's powerhouse that, among other tasks, converts nutrients to energy). They found that a cascade of reactions triggered by lower caloric intake raises the levels of these enzymes, leading to an increase in the strength and efficiency of the cellular batteries. By invigorating the mitochondria, SIRT3 and SIRT4 extend the life of cells, by preventing flagging mitochondria from developing tiny holes (or pores) in their membranes that allow proteins that trigger apoptosis, or cell death, to seep out into the rest of the cell.

"We didn't expect that the most important part of this pathway was in the mitochondria," says David Sinclair, an assistant professor of pathology at Harvard Medical School and a study co-author. "We think that we've possibly found regulators of aging."

In 2003 Sinclair's lab published a paper in *Nature* that described the discovery of a gene that switched on in the yeast cell in response to calorie restriction, which Sinclair calls a "master regulator in aging." Since then, his team has been searching for an analogous gene that plays a similar role in the mammalian cell.

The researchers determined from cultures of human embryonic kidney cells that lower caloric intake sends a signal that activates a gene inside cells that codes for the enzyme NAMPT (nicotinamide phosphoribosyltransferase). The two- to four-fold surge in NAMPT in turn triggers the production of a molecule called NAD (nicotinamide adenine dinucleotide), which plays a key role in cellular metabolism and signaling.

The uptick in NAD levels activates the *SIRT3* and *SIRT4* genes, increasing levels of their corresponding SIRT3 and SIRT4 enzymes, which then flood the interior of the mitochondria. Sinclair says he's not sure exactly how SIRT3 and SIRT4 beef up the mitochondria's energy output, but that events leading to cell death are at the very least delayed when there are vast quantities of the enzymes.

SIRT3 and SIRT4 are part of a family called sirtuins. (SIRT1, which helps extend cell life by modulating the number of repair proteins fixing DNA damage both inside and outside the cell's nucleus is also a member.) SIRT is short for sir-2 homologue–a well-studied protein that is known to extend yeast cell longevity. According to Sinclair, all of the mammalian *SIRT* genes (and their proteins) are possible drug targets for therapies aimed at extending life, as well as staving off age-related illnesses, such as Alzheimer's disease, cancers, and metabolic disorders like diabetes.

"I think *SIRT3* is the next most interesting sirtuin from a drug development standpoint," Sinclair says. "It does protect cells, but there's growing evidence that it may mediate the benefits of exercise as well."

Sinclair's lab is now working on developing what he calls a possible "supermouse" with elevated levels of NAMPT to see if it lives longer and is more disease-resistant than normal mice.

Matt Kaeberlein, a pathologist at the University of Washington in Seattle, says that Sinclair's team has an interesting hypothesis connecting the mitochondria to longevity, but that it needs to be more directly tested in the context of dietary restriction. "If the NAMPT-overexpressing mice are long-lived and disease resistant, that will provide more support for this idea."

For his part, Sinclair is eager to see the results of his experiments with the supermouse. "Depending on how this mouse turns out," he says, "we may put NAMPT on the list of drug targets, as well."

Why the Life Expectancy Gap between Men and Women Is Growing

By Lori Youmshajekian

Women have outlived men for more than a century in the U.S. Demographers have largely attributed this well-known statistical gap to differences in behaviors in areas such as smoking and drinking habits, risk of injury, and drug use. Overall U.S. life expectancy had been slowly improving for decades, but data from the Centers for Disease Control and Prevention show some of this progress has recently been overturned—especially among men.

In 2010 women were projected to live 4.8 years longer than men. By 2021 this gap widened to 5.8 years, the largest disparity since 1996. During the 20th century, heart disease was the main cause of death that created the difference in life expectancy among women and men. But now COVID fatalities and a growing number of drug overdoses among men are to blame, according to a new analysis of CDC data published in *JAMA Internal Medicine*. (The report designated gender based on binary gender data that were recorded in death certificates.)

A greater number of COVID deaths among men—influenced by a higher burden of comorbidities, differences in health behaviors, and employment in higher-risk industries—was a big part of the "deeply troubling" drop in life expectancy and widening gender gap, says Philip Cohen, a professor of sociology at the University of Maryland, who was not involved in the study. "But this report underscores some underlying public health problems that also disproportionately affect men, especially drug overdoses, suicide, and other violence."

Before the pandemic, in the years between 2010 and 2019, the largest contributor to the gap was the category of unintentional injuries—mostly drug overdoses but also transport-related injuries such as car accidents. Other factors included rising rates of diabetes, suicides, homicides, and heart disease. All of these increased the life expectancy gap by 0.23 year.

The most substantial change in projected life expectancy at birth occurred between 2019 and 2021: the onset of the COVID pandemic. Death from the widespread illness was a major factor in decreasing men's average life expectancy to 73.2 years in this period, compared with 79.1 years in women. This was on top of already higher rates of death from unintentional injuries–which were, again, overwhelmingly drug overdoses.

The discrepancy is "unsettling," says Brandon Yan, lead author of the new analysis. Overall life expectancy has been declining since COVID–from 78.8 years in 2019 to 76.1 years in 2021–"which is concerning in and of itself," says Yan, a resident physician at the University of California, San Francisco, School of Medicine, and a research collaborator at the Harvard T. H. Chan School of Public Health.

Yan and his colleagues were initially surprised that men had a disproportionate COVID mortality burden. "Part of the [reason] is men, on average, are sicker than women" when they contract COVID, he says.

Sarah Richardson, who directs the GenderSci Lab at Harvard University and was not involved in the study, says the findings were consistent with her previous research that found a small increase in COVID mortality among men, compared with women. "So the results are not surprising from that perspective," Richardson says. The trend was even more pronounced in younger populations, she adds.

Deaths at a younger age have an exaggerated effect on life expectancy calculations, says Elizabeth Wrigley-Field, an associate professor of sociology at the University of Minnesota, who did not participate in the recent research. Most people who die from opioid overdose, for example, should have had decades left to live, she says. "That's why each of those deaths can really affect the population lifespan or life expectancy in a meaningful way," Wrigley-Field adds, "more so than for causes of death that tend to kill people at much older ages."

The gender gap was slightly offset by improvements in cancer survival rates in men, as well as worsening rates of maternal deaths—a growing public health problem nationwide. "It's similarly something that has a profound, disproportionate impact on life expectancy," Wrigley-Field says, "because the women are at a relatively young age, when they should have had many decades to live."

Previous research has attributed biological factors, such as a more robust immune system, to women's relative longevity. But this cannot explain such a significant change in life expectancy in the span of the analysis from 2010 to 2021, Yan says. The changes over such a short period come down to increasing rates of chronic disease burden among men and the worsening mental health crisis, he says.

The reason why COVID and overdose-related mortality had worsened to such an extent among men might have to do with occupation and health-care access, Richardson says. She adds that masculinity norms and pressures may prevent some men from complaining that they're in pain or in need of care. "It is much less likely for men to appear for care before a situation is very acute, and so they have poorer outcomes," she says. Yan adds that risk factors such as being unhoused or working in construction or agriculture—both situations in which men constitute the overwhelming majority—have been associated with increased exposure to COVID.

Donald Miller, an epidemiologist at the Boston University School of Public Health and a co-author of the new analysis, says persuading more older men to get vaccinations would improve the life expectancy trend. But, he adds, "the bigger challenge is younger men." More research into the reasons behind men's riskier health behaviors is needed to develop better interventions for drug misuse, violence, and suicide. Cohen says preventative care, mental health care and earlier detection would help alleviate these areas.

The recent analysis used death certificate data, which lack specificity beyond a binary gender classification. The report also didn't account for location, race, or socioeconomic factors—which Richardson says may reveal vast discrepancies among those subgroups. Her previous analysis of COVID deaths, for instance, showed mortality rates varied significantly on a state-by-state level. Yan is awaiting the release of life expectancy data for 2022 later this month and hopes the additional information will help future studies on demographic factors that may influence the gender disparity.

The trends that reflect more deaths among men and countervailing trends such as increased maternal mortality are happening in the U.S.—which has a significantly higher overall mortality rate than its peer countries, Wrigley-Field says. "The right starting point for asking why any particular group in the U.S. has such high mortality is to ask why the entire United States does," she says.

The answer isn't simple; poverty, overwork, a lack of safety nets, a fragmented medical system, and daily stressors could all play a role. But the truth is probably something like "all of the above," Wrigley-Field says.

"These trends should be a wake-up call that we can't coast along toward better and longer lives," Cohen says. "We need real, substantial and sustained attention to public health and health care in this country—and we need it yesterday."

If You Need Help

If you or someone you know is struggling or having thoughts of suicide, help is available. Call or text the 988 Suicide & Crisis Lifeline at 988 or use the online Lifeline Chat.

About the Author

Lori Youmshajekian is a freelance science journalist who reports on advances in health, environmental issues and scientific misconduct. She holds a master's degree in Science Journalism from New York University and has written for New Scientist, Yale E360, Retraction Watch and Medscape, among other outlets.

Section 5: Cheating Death and Life After Death

Is Death Reversible?

By Christof Koch

"And death shall have no dominion" –Dylan Thomas, 1933

You will die, sooner or later. We all will. For everything that has a beginning has an end, an ineluctable consequence of the second law of thermodynamics.

Few of us like to think about this troubling fact. But once birthed, the thought of oblivion can't be completely erased. It lurks in the unconscious shadows, ready to burst forth. In my case, it was only as a mature man that I became fully mortal. I had wasted an entire evening playing an addictive, first-person shooter video game–running through subterranean halls, flooded corridors, nightmarishly turning tunnels, and empty plazas under a foreign sun, firing my weapons at hordes of aliens relentlessly pursuing me. I went to bed, easily falling asleep but awoke abruptly a few hours later. Abstract knowledge had turned to felt reality–I was going to die! Not right there and then but eventually.

Evolution equipped our species with powerful defense mechanisms to deal with this foreknowledge–in particular, psychological suppression and religion. The former prevents us from consciously acknowledging or dwelling on such uncomfortable truths while the latter reassures us by promising never-ending life in a Christian heaven, an eternal cycle of Buddhist reincarnations, or an uploading of our mind to the Cloud, the 21st-century equivalent of rapture for nerds.

Death has no such dominion over nonhuman animals. Although they can grieve for dead offspring and companions, there is no credible evidence that apes, dogs, crows and bees have minds sufficiently self-aware to be troubled by the insight that one day they will be no more. Thus, these defense mechanisms must have arisen in recent hominin evolution, in less than 10 million years.

Teachings from religious and philosophical traditions have long emphasized the opposite: look squarely into the hollow eyes of death to remove its sting. Daily meditation on nonbeing lessens its terror. As a scientist with intimations of my own mortality, my reflections turn toward understanding what death is.

Anyone who undertakes this quest will soon come to realize that death, this looming presence just over the horizon, is quite ill defined from both a scientific as well as a medical point of view.

From the Chest to the Head

Throughout history, everyone knew what death was. When somebody stopped breathing and their heart ceased beating for more than a few minutes, the person was, quite simply, dead. Death was a well-demarcated moment in time. All of this changed with the advent of mechanical ventilators and cardiac pacemakers in the middle of the 20th century. Modern high-tech intensive care decoupled the heart and the lungs from the brain that is responsible for mind, thought, and action.

In response to these technological developments, in 1968, the famous *Report of the Ad Hoc Committee of the Harvard Medical School* introduced the concept of death as irreversible coma–that is, loss of brain function. This adjustment was given the force of law by the Uniform Determination of Death Act in 1981. This document defines death as either irreversible cessation of circulatory and respiratory functions or irreversible halting of brain function. Quite simply, when your brain is dead, you are dead.

This definition is, by and large, in use throughout most of the advanced world. The locus of death shifted from the chest to the brain (and from public view into the private sphere of the hospital room), with the exact time of actual brain death uncertain. This rapid and widespread acceptance of brain death, reaffirmed by a presidential commission in 2008, is remarkable when compared with the ongoing controversy around abortion and the beginning of life. It may perhaps be reflective of another little noticed asymmetry–people agonize about what happens in the hereafter but rarely about where they were before being born!

The vast majority of deaths still occur following cardiopulmonary cessation, which then terminates brain functioning as well. Neurological death–specified by irreversible coma, absence of responses, brain stem reflexes or respiration—is uncommon beyond the intensive care unit, where patients with traumatic or anoxic brain injury or toxic-metabolic coma (say, following an opioid overdose) are typically admitted.

Brain death may be the defining factor, but that does not simplify clinical diagnosis—biological processes can persist after the brain shuts down. Indeed, a brain-dead body can be kept "alive" or on "life support" for hours, days or longer. For the grieving relatives and friends, it is challenging to understand what is happening. When visiting the ICU, they see the chest moving in and out, they feel a pulse, the skin pallor looks normal, and the body is warm. Looking healthier than some of the other denizens of the ICU, their beloved is now legally a corpse, a beating-heart cadaver. The body is ventilated and kept suspended in this quasi-living state because it is now a potential organ donor. If permission has been obtained, the organs can be harvested from the cadaver to help the living who need a heart, kidney, liver, or lung, which are always in short supply.

Brain-dead bodies can continue to grow fingernails, to menstruate, with at least some working immune function that allows them to fight off infections. There are more than 30 known cases of pregnant brain-dead mothers placed on a ventilator to support gestation of a surviving fetus, born weeks or months (in one case 107 days) after the mother became brain-dead. In a widely discussed 2018 story in the *New Yorker*, a young woman, Jahi McMath, was maintained on ventilation in a home care setting in New Jersey by her family following her brain death in a hospital in California. To the law and established medical consensus, she was dead. To her loving family, she was alive for close to five years until she died from bleeding associated with liver failure.

Despite technological advances, biology and medicine still lack a coherent and principled understanding of what precisely defines birth and death—the two bookends that delimit life. Aristotle wrote in *De anima* more than two millennia ago that any living body is more than the sum of its parts. He taught that the vegetative soul of any organism, whether a plant, animal, or person, is the form or the essence of this living thing.

The essence of a vegetative soul encompasses its powers of nutrition, growth, and reproduction that depend on the body. When these vital capacities are gone, the organism ceases to be animate (a term whose roots lead back to *anima*, Latin for "soul"). The sensitive soul mediates the capacities of both animals and humans to sense the world and their bodies. It is the closest to what we moderns call "conscious experience." Finally, the rational soul is the sole province of people, mediating reason, language, and speech. Of course, this is now increasingly mimicked by artificial-intelligence algorithms.

The modern emphasis on machine learning, genomics, proteomics, and big data provides the illusion of understanding what the vegetative soul is. Yet it obscures the depth of our ignorance about what explains the breakdown of the vegetative soul. A conceptual challenge remains to define what constitutes anyone's living body—which is clearly more than the sum of its individual organs. How can one precisely delimit this body in space (are clothing, dental implants, and contact lenses part of the body?) and in time (its beginning and its end)?

Note the word "irreversible" in the contemporary definition of neurological death. In the absence of a precise conceptual formulation of when an organism is alive or dead, the concept of irreversibility depends on the technology *du jour*, which is constantly evolving. What at the beginning of the 20th century was irreversible—cessation of breathing—became reversible by the end of the century. Is it too difficult to contemplate that the same may be true for brain death? A recent experiment suggests this idea is not just a wild imagining.

Partial Revival of Dead Brains

This year a large team of physicians and scientists at the Yale School of Medicine under Nenad Sestan took advantage of hundreds of pigs killed at a Department of Agriculture–approved slaughterhouse for a remarkable experiment, published in the journal *Nature*. The researchers removed the brains from their skulls and connected the carotid arteries and veins to a perfusion device that mimics a beating heart. It circulates a kind of artificial blood, a synthetic mixture of compounds that carry oxygen and drugs that protect cells from damage. The magic resides in the exact molecular constitution of the circulating solution. Think of closed-circuit dialysis machines that thousands of patients use daily to flush out toxins from their body because their own kidneys have stopped working.

These machines are needed because when blood stops flowing through the large, energy-demanding brain, oxygen stores are depleted within seconds, and consciousness is lost. Depriving a brain of oxygen and blood flow for more than a few minutes begins to trigger irreversible damage. Cells start degenerating in all sorts of ways (tissue damage and decomposition, edema, and so on) that are readily visible under a microscope.

The Sestan team studied the brains' viability four hours after the pigs were electrically stunned, bled out, and decapitated. (If this sounds gruesome, it is what happens to livestock in an abattoir, one reason I'm a vegetarian.) The researchers compared a variety of biological indicators with those of postmortem control brains from pigs that did not undergo this perfusion procedure four hours after death, an eternity for the sensitive nervous system.

At first glance, the restored brains with the circulating solution appeared relatively normal. As the compound circulated, the fine net of arteries, capillaries, and veins that suffuse brain tissue responded appropriately; the tissue integrity was preserved with a reduction in swelling that leads to cell death; synapses, neurons, and their output wires (axons) looked normal. Glial cells, the underappreciated entities supporting neurons proper, showed some functionality, and the brain consumed oxygen and glucose, the universal energy currency of the body, an indication of some metabolic functioning. The title of the researchers' paper announcing their technology boldly states "Restoration of Brain Circulation and Cellular Functions Hours Post-mortem."

What was not present in these results were brain waves of the kind familiar from electroencephalographic (EEG) recordings. Electrodes placed onto the surface of the pig brains measured no spontaneous global electrical activity: none of the deep-slow waves that march in lockstep across the cerebral cortex during deep sleep, no abrupt paroxysm of electrical activity followed by silence—what is known as burst suppression. Only a flat line everywhere—a global isoelectric line—

implying a complete absence of any sort of consciousness. A silent brain, electrically speaking, is not harboring an experiencing mind. But this was not a surprise. This state was exactly what was intended by Sestan and his coworkers, which is why the circulating solution contained a cocktail of drugs that suppresses neuronal function and corresponding synaptic communication among cells.

Even with the absence of brain waves it came as a surprise to me, a working neuroscientist, that individual pig cortical neurons still retained their capacity to generate electrical and synaptic activity. The Yale team demonstrated this by snipping a tiny sliver of neural tissue from these brains, washing off the perfused solution and then exciting individual neurons via an electric current delivered by a tiny electrode. Some of these cells responded appropriately by generating one or a series of the stereotypical electrical pulses, so-called action potentials or spikes, that are the universal idiom of rapid communication in any advanced nervous system.

This finding raises a profound question: What would happen if the team were to remove the neural-activity blockers from the solution suffusing the brain? Most likely nothing. Just because some individual neurons retain some potential for excitability does not imply that millions and millions of neurons can spontaneously self-organize and break out into an electrical chorus. And yet! It cannot be ruled out that with some kind of external help, a sort of cortical defibrillator, these "dead" brains could be booted up, reviving the brain rhythms characteristic of the living brain.

To state the obvious, decapitating any sentient creature and letting its brain bleed out is not conducive to its well-being. Reanimating it after such a major trauma could well lead to profound pathology, such as massive epileptic seizures, delirium, deep-seated pain, distress, psychosis, and so on. No creature should ever suffer in this manner. It is precisely to avoid this situation that the Yale team obstructed neuronal function.

This brings me to the elephant in the room. Can this procedure be applied to the human brain? Before you recoil, think of the following. What would you want done if your child or partner were found drowned or overdosed, without a pulse or breath for hours? Today it is likely that they would be declared dead. Could this change tomorrow with the kind of technology pioneered by the Yale group? Isn't that a worthwhile goal to pursue?

The pig brain is a large brain, unlike the one of the much smaller mouse, by far the most popular laboratory animal. Pig cortex is highly folded, like the human cortex. Neurosurgical procedures are routinely tested on pigs before moving to human trials. So, the technical answer is yes; in principle, this could be done.

But should it be done?

Certainly not until we understand much better whether a reconstituted animal brain shows global electrical activity typical of a healthy brain, without stress responses indicative of pain, distress, or agony. The field as a whole should pause and discuss the medical, scientific, legal, ethical, philosophical, and political questions of such research with all stakeholders.

Yet the fear of the grim reaper will not be denied. Sooner or later, somewhere on the planet's face, someone will try to temporarily cheat death.

Referenced

The Undead: Organ Harvesting, the Ice-Water Test, Beating-Heart Cadavers—How Medicine Is Blurring the Line between Life and Death. Dick Teresi. Pantheon, 2012.

Modern Death: How Medicine Changed the End of Life. Haider Warraich. St. Martin's Press, 2017.

"Restoration of Brain Circulation and Cellular Functions Hours Post-mortem." Zvonimir Vrselja et al. in *Nature*, Vol. 568, pages 336–343; April 18, 2019.

About the Author

Christof Koch is a neuroscientist at the Allen Institute and at the Tiny Blue Dot Foundation, the former president of the Allen Institute for Brain Science, and a former professor at the California Institute of Technology. His latest book is Then I Am Myself the World. *Koch writes regularly for a range of media, including* Scientific American. *He lives in the Pacific Northwest.*

Never Say Die: Why We Can't Imagine Death

By Jesse Bering

Everybody's wonderin' what and where they all came from. Everybody's worryin' 'bout where they're gonna go when the whole thing's done. But no one knows for certain and so it's all the same to me. I think I'll just let the mystery be.

It should strike us as odd that we feel inclined to nod our heads in agreement to the twangy, sweetly discordant folk vocals of Iris Dement in "Let the Mystery Be," a humble paean about the hereafter. In fact, the only real mystery is why we're so convinced that when it comes to where we're going "when the whole thing's done," we're dealing with a mystery at all. After all, the brain is like any other organ: a part of our physical body. And the mind is what the brain does–it's more a verb than it is a noun. Why do we wonder where our mind goes when the body is dead? Shouldn't it be obvious that the mind is dead too?

And yet people in every culture believe in an afterlife of some kind or, at the very least, are unsure about what happens to the mind at death. My psychological research has led me to believe that these irrational beliefs, rather than resulting from religion or serving to protect us from the terror of inexistence, are an inevitable by-product of self-consciousness. Because we have never experienced a lack of consciousness, we cannot imagine what it will feel like to be dead. In fact, it won't feel like anything–and therein lies the problem.

The common view of death as a great mystery usually is brushed aside as an emotionally fueled desire to believe that death isn't the end of the road. And indeed, a prominent school of research in social psychology called terror management theory contends that afterlife beliefs, as well as less obvious beliefs, behaviors, and attitudes, exist to assuage what would otherwise be crippling anxiety about the ego's inexistence.

According to proponents, you possess a secret arsenal of psychological defenses designed to keep your death anxiety at bay (and to keep you from ending up in the fetal position listening to Nick Drake on your iPod). My writing this article, for example, would be interpreted as an exercise in "symbolic immortality"; terror management theorists would likely tell you that I wrote it for posterity, to enable a concrete set of my ephemeral ideas to outlive me, the biological organism. (I would tell you that I'd be happy enough if a year from now it still had a faint pulse.)

Yet a small number of researchers, including me, are increasingly arguing that the evolution of self-consciousness has posed a different kind of problem altogether. This position holds that our ancestors suffered the unshakable illusion that their minds were immortal, and it's this hiccup of gross irrationality that we have unmistakably inherited from them. Individual human beings, by virtue of their evolved cognitive architecture, had trouble conceptualizing their own psychological inexistence from the start.

Curiously Immortal

The problem applies even to those who claim not to believe in an afterlife. As philosopher and Center for Naturalism founder Thomas W. Clark wrote in a 1994 article for the *Humanist* (emphases mine):

> Here ... is the view at issue: When we die, what's next is *nothing*; death is an abyss, a black hole, the end of experience; it is eternal nothingness, the permanent extinction of being. And here, in a nutshell, is the error contained in that view: It is to *reify* nothingness–make it a positive condition or quality (for example, of "blackness")–and then to place the individual in it after death, so that we somehow fall *into* nothingness, to remain there eternally.

Consider the rather startling fact that you will never know you have died. You may feel yourself slipping away, but it isn't as though there will be a "you" around who is capable of ascertaining that, once all is said and done, it has actually happened. Just to remind you, you need a working cerebral cortex to harbor propositional knowledge of any sort, including the fact that you've died—and once you've died your brain is about as phenomenally generative as a head of lettuce. In a 2007 article published in the journal *Synthese*, University of Arizona philosopher Shaun Nichols puts it this way: "When I try to imagine my own non-existence I have to imagine that I perceive or know about my non-existence. No wonder there's an obstacle!"

This observation may not sound like a major revelation to you, but I bet you've never considered what it actually means, which is that your own mortality is unfalsifiable from the first-person perspective. This obstacle is why writer Johann Wolfgang von Goethe allegedly remarked that "everyone carries the proof of his own immortality within himself."

Even when we want to believe that our minds end at death, it is a real struggle to think in this way. A study I published in the *Journal of Cognition and Culture* in 2002 reveals the illusion of immortality operating in full swing in the minds of undergraduate students who were asked a series of questions about the psychological faculties of a dead man.

Richard, I told the students, had been killed instantaneously when his vehicle plunged into a utility pole. After the participants read a narrative about Richard's state of mind just prior to the accident, I queried them as to whether the man, now that he was dead, retained the capacity to experience mental states. "Is Richard still thinking about his wife?" I asked them. "Can he still taste the flavor of the breath mint he ate just before he died? Does he want to be alive?"

You can imagine the looks I got, because apparently not many people pause to consider whether souls have taste buds, become randy, or get headaches. Yet most gave answers indicative of "psychological continuity reasoning," in which they envisioned Richard's mind to continue functioning despite his death. This finding came as no surprise given that, on a separate scale, most respondents classified themselves as having a belief in some form of an afterlife.

What *was* surprising, however, was that many participants who had identified themselves as having "extinctivist" beliefs (they had ticked off the box that read: "What we think of as the 'soul,' or conscious personality of a person, ceases permanently when the body dies") occasionally gave psychological-continuity responses, too. Thirty-two percent of the extinctivists' answers betrayed their hidden reasoning that emotions and desires survive death; another 36 percent of their responses suggested the extinctivists reasoned this way for mental states related to knowledge (such as remembering, believing or knowing). One particularly vehement extinctivist thought the whole line of questioning silly and seemed to regard me as a numbskull for even asking. But just as well—he proceeded to point out that of course Richard knows he is dead, because there's no afterlife and Richard sees that now.

So why is it so hard to conceptualize inexistence anyway? Part of my own account, which I call the "simulation constraint hypothesis," is that in attempting to imagine what it's like to be dead we appeal to our own background of conscious experiences—because that's how we approach most thought experiments. Death isn't "like" anything we've ever experienced, however. Because we have never consciously been without consciousness, even our best simulations of true nothingness just aren't good enough.

For us extinctivists, it's kind of like staring into a hallway of mirrors—but rather than confronting a visual trick, we're dealing with cognitive reverberations of subjective experience. In Spanish philosopher Miguel de Unamuno's 1913 existential screed, *The Tragic Sense of Life*, one can almost see the author tearing out his hair contemplating this very fact. "Try to fill your consciousness with the representation of no-consciousness," he writes, "and you will see the impossibility of it. The effort to comprehend it causes the most tormenting dizziness."

Wait, you say, isn't Unamuno forgetting something? We certainly do have experience with nothingness. Every night, in fact, when we're in dreamless sleep. But you'd be mistaken in this assumption. Clark puts it this way (emphasis mine): "We may occasionally have the *impression* of having experienced or 'undergone' a period of unconsciousness, but, of course, this is impossible. The 'nothingness' of unconsciousness cannot be an experienced actuality."

If psychological immortality represents the intuitive, natural way of thinking about death, then we might expect young children to be particularly inclined to reason in this way. As an eight-year-old, I watched as the remains of our family's golden retriever, Sam, were buried in the woods behind our house. Still, I thought Sam had a mind capable of knowing I loved her and I was sorry I didn't get to say goodbye. That Sam's spirit lived on was not something my parents or anyone else ever explicitly pointed out to me. Although she had been reduced to no more than a few ounces of dust, which was in turn sealed in a now waterlogged box, it never even occurred to me that it was a strange idea.

Yet if you were to have asked me what Sam was experiencing, I probably would have muttered something like the type of answers Gerald P. Koocher reported hearing in a 1973 study published in *Developmental Psychology*. Koocher, then a doctoral student at the University of Missouri–Columbia and later president of the American Psychological Association, asked six- to 15-year-olds what happens when you die. Consistent with the simulation-constraint hypothesis, many answers relied on everyday experience to describe death, "with references to sleeping, feeling 'peaceful,' or simply 'being very dizzy.' "

A Mind-Body Disconnect

But Koocher's study in itself doesn't tell us where such ideas come from. The simulation-constraint hypothesis posits that this type of thinking is innate and unlearned. Fortunately, this hypothesis is falsifiable. If afterlife beliefs are a product of cultural indoctrination, with children picking up such ideas through religious teachings, through the media, or informally through family and friends, then one should rationally predict that psychological-continuity reasoning *increases* with age. Aside from becoming more aware of their own mortality, after all, older kids have had a longer period of exposure to the concept of an afterlife.

In fact, recent findings show the opposite developmental trend. In a 2004 study reported in *Developmental Psychology*, Florida Atlantic University psychologist David F. Bjorklund and I presented 200 three- to 12-year-olds with a puppet show. Every child saw the story of Baby Mouse, who was out strolling innocently in the woods. "Just then," we told them, "he notices something very strange. The bushes are moving! An alligator jumps out of the bushes and gobbles him all up. Baby Mouse is not alive anymore."

Just like the adults from the previously mentioned study, the children were asked about dead Baby Mouse's psychological functioning. "Does Baby Mouse still want to go home?" we asked them. "Does he still feel sick?" "Can he still smell the flowers?" The youngest children in the study, the three- to five-year-olds, were significantly more likely to reason in terms of psychological continuity than children from the two older age groups were.

But here's the really curious part. Even the preschoolers had a solid grasp on biological cessation; they knew, for example, that dead Baby Mouse didn't need food or water anymore. They knew he wouldn't grow up to be an adult mouse. Heck, 85 percent of the youngest kids even told us that his brain no longer worked. Yet most of these very young children then told us that dead Baby Mouse was hungry or thirsty, that he felt better or that he was still angry at his brother.

One couldn't say that the preschoolers lacked a concept of death, therefore, because nearly all of the kids realized that biological imperatives no longer applied after death. Rather they seemed to have trouble using this knowledge to theorize about related mental functions.

From an evolutionary perspective, a coherent theory about psychological death is not necessarily vital. Anthropologist H. Clark Barrett of the University of California, Los Angeles, believes instead that understanding the cessation of "agency" (for example, that a dead creature isn't going to suddenly leap up and bite you) is probably what saved lives (and thus genes). According to Barrett, comprehending the cessation of the mind, on the other hand, has no survival value and is, in an evolutionary sense, unnecessary.

In a 2005 study published in the journal *Cognition*, Barrett and psychologist Tanya Behne of the University of Manchester in England reported that city-dwelling four-year-olds from Berlin were just as good at distinguishing sleeping animals from dead ones as hunter-horticulturalist children from the Shuar region of Ecuador were. Even today's urban children appear tuned in to perceptual cues signaling death. A "violation of the body envelope" (in other words, a mutilated carcass) is a pretty good sign that one needn't worry about tiptoeing around.

The Culture Factor

On the one hand, then, from a very early age, children realize that dead bodies are not coming back to life. On the other hand, also from a very early age, kids endow the dead with ongoing psychological functions. So where do culture and religious teaching come into the mix, if at all?

In fact, exposure to the concept of an afterlife plays a crucial role in enriching and elaborating this natural cognitive stance; it's sort of like an architectural scaffolding process, whereby culture develops and decorates the innate psychological building blocks of religious belief. The end product can be as ornate or austere as you like, from the headache-inducing reincarnation beliefs of Theravada Buddhists to the man on the street's "I believe there's *something*" brand of philosophy—but it's made of the same brick and mortar just the same.

In support of the idea that culture influences our natural tendency to deny the death of the mind, Harvard University psychologist Paul Harris and researcher Marta Giménez of the National University of Distance Education in Spain showed that when the wording in interviews is tweaked to include medical or scientific terms, psychological-continuity reasoning decreases. In this 2005 study published in the *Journal of Cognition and Culture*, seven- to 11-year-old children in Madrid who heard a story about a priest telling a child that his grandmother "is with God" were more likely to attribute ongoing mental states to the decedent than were those who heard the identical story but instead about a doctor saying a grandfather was "dead and buried."

And in a 2005 replication of the Baby Mouse experiment published in the *British Journal of Developmental Psychology*, psychologist David Bjorklund and I teamed with psychologist Carlos Hernández Blasi of Jaume I University in Spain to compare children in a Catholic school with those attending a public secular school in Castellón, Spain. As in the previous study, an overwhelming majority of the youngest children—five- to six-year-olds—from both educational backgrounds said that Baby Mouse's mental states survived. The type of curriculum, secular or religious, made no difference. With increasing age, however, culture becomes a factor—the kids attending Catholic school were more likely to reason in terms of psychological continuity than were those at the secular school. There was even a smattering of young extinctivists in the latter camp.

Free Spirits

The types of cognitive obstacles discussed earlier may be responsible for our innate sense of immortality. But although the simulation-constraint hypothesis helps to explain why so many people believe in something as fantastically illogical as an afterlife, it doesn't tell us why people see the soul unbuckling itself from the body and floating off like an invisible helium balloon into the realm of eternity. After all, there's nothing to stop us from having afterlife beliefs that involve the still active mind being entombed in the skull and deliriously happy. Yet almost nobody has such a belief.

Back when you were still in diapers, you learned that people didn't cease to exist simply because you couldn't see them. Developmental psychologists even have a fancy term for this basic concept: "person permanence." Such an off-line social awareness leads us to tacitly assume that the people we know are *somewhere* doing *something*. As I'm writing this article in Belfast, for example, my mind's eye conjures up my friend Ginger in New Orleans walking her poodle or bickering with her husband, things that I know she does routinely.

As I've argued in my 2006 *Behavioral and Brain Sciences* article, "The Folk Psychology of Souls," human cognition is not equipped to update the list of players in our complex social rosters by accommodating a particular person's sudden inexistence. We can't simply switch off our person-permanence thinking just because someone has died. This inability is especially the case, of course, for those whom we were closest to and whom we frequently imagined to be actively engaging in various activities when out of sight.

And so person permanence may be the final cognitive hurdle that gets in the way of our effectively realizing the dead as they truly are–infinitely in situ, inanimate carbon residue. Instead it's much more "natural" to imagine them as existing in some vague, unobservable locale, very much living their dead lives.

Referenced

"Intuitive Conceptions of Dead Agents' Minds: The Natural Foundations of Afterlife Beliefs as Phenomenological Boundary." Jesse M. Bering in *Journal of Cognition and Culture*, Vol. 2, No. 4, pages 263–308; 2002.

"The Natural Emergence of Reasoning about the Afterlife as a Developmental Regularity." Jesse M. Bering and David Bjorklund in *Developmental Psychology*, Vol. 40, pages 217–233; 2004.

"The Folk Psychology of Souls." Jesse M. Bering in *Behavioral and Brain Sciences*, Vol. 29, No. 5, pages 453–498; October 2006.

About the Author

Jesse Bering is Associate Professor of Science Communication at the University of Otago in New Zealand. He is the author of The Belief Instinct *(2011),* Why Is the Penis Shaped Like That? *(2012) and* Perv *(2013). To learn more about Jesse's work, visit www.jessebering.com or add him on Facebook (https://www.facebook.com/jesse.bering).*

Why the "You" in an Afterlife Wouldn't Really Be You

By Michael Shermer

The Discovery is a 2017 Netflix film in which Robert Redford plays a scientist who proves that the afterlife is real. "Once the body dies, some part of our consciousness leaves us and travels to a new plane," the scientist explains, evidenced by his machine that measures, as another character puts it, "brain wavelengths on a subatomic level leaving the body after death."

This idea is not too far afield from a real theory called quantum consciousness, proffered by a wide range of people, from physicist Roger Penrose to physician Deepak Chopra. Some versions hold that our mind is not strictly the product of our brain and that consciousness exists separately from material substance, so the death of your physical body is not the end of your conscious existence. Because this is the topic of my next book, *Heavens on Earth: The Scientific Search for the Afterlife, Immortality, and Utopia* (Henry Holt, 2018), the film triggered a number of problems I have identified with all such concepts, both scientific and religious.

First, there is the assumption that our identity is located in our memories, which are presumed to be permanently recorded in the brain: if they could be copied and pasted into a computer or duplicated and implanted into a resurrected body or soul, we would be restored. But that is not how memory works. Memory is not like a DVR that can play back the past on a screen in your mind. Memory is a continually edited and fluid process that utterly depends on the neurons in your brain being functional. It is true that when you go to sleep and wake up the next morning or go under anesthesia for surgery and come back hours later, your memories return, as they do even after so-called profound hypothermia and circulatory arrest. Under this procedure, a patient's brain is cooled to as low as 50 degrees Fahrenheit, which causes electrical activity in neurons to stop—suggesting that long-term memories are stored statically. But that cannot happen if your brain dies. That is why CPR has to be done so soon after a heart attack or drowning—because if the brain is starved of oxygen-rich blood, the neurons die, along with the memories stored therein.

Second, there is the supposition that copying your brain's connectome—the diagram of its neural connections—uploading it into a computer (as some scientists suggest) or resurrecting your physical self in an afterlife (as many religions envision) will result in you waking up as if from a long sleep either in a lab or in heaven. But a copy of your memories, your mind, or even your soul is not you. It is a *copy* of you, no different than a twin, and no twin looks at their sibling and thinks, "There I am." Neither duplication nor resurrection can instantiate you in another plane of existence.

Third, your unique identity is more than just your intact memories; it is also your personal point of view. Neuroscientist Kenneth Hayworth, a senior scientist at the Howard Hughes Medical Institute and president of the Brain Preservation Foundation, divided this entity into the MEMself and the POVself. He believes that if a complete MEMself is transferred into a computer (or, presumably, resurrected in heaven), the POVself will awaken. I disagree. If this were done without the death of the person, there would be two memory selves, each with its own POVself looking out at the world through its unique eyes. At that moment, each would take a different path in life, thereby recording different memories based on different experiences. "You" would not suddenly have two POVs. If you died, there is no known mechanism by which your POVself would be transported from your brain into a computer (or a resurrected body). A POV depends entirely on the continuity of self from one moment to the next, even if that continuity is broken by sleep or anesthesia. Death is a permanent break in continuity, and your personal POV cannot be moved from your brain into some other medium, here or in the hereafter.

If this sounds dispiriting, it is just the opposite. Awareness of our mortality is uplifting because it means that every moment, every day and every relationship matters. Engaging deeply with the world and with other sentient beings brings meaning and purpose. We are each of us unique in the world and in history, geographically and chronologically. Our genomes and connectomes cannot be duplicated, so we are individuals vouchsafed with awareness of our mortality and self-awareness of what that means. What does it mean? Life is not some temporary staging before the big show hereafter–it is our personal proscenium in the drama of the cosmos here and now.

About the Author

Michael Shermer is publisher of Skeptic *magazine (www.skeptic.com) and a Presidential Fellow at Chapman University. His new book is* Heavens on Earth: The Scientific Search for the Afterlife, Immortality, and Utopia *(Henry Holt, 2018).*

Can AI Predict Your Death?

By Lauren Leffer, Elah Feder, and Tulika Bose

A new study used machine learning to "autocomplete" the life trajectories of 6 million Danish people—and forecast when they might kick the bucket.

Lauren Leffer: Prediction is powerful. For as long as people have been thinking about the future, we've been trying to predict it. And, in some areas, we've gotten pretty good (think, like, meteorology and climate modeling).

Tulika Bose: But scientifically speaking—we're still pretty far from the stuff of crystal balls and oracles. There's lots of things people have no reliable way to forecast, despite what your horoscope may suggest.

Leffer: Absolutely. But... what if artificial intelligence could get us closer to that fantasy/supernatural realm of divination than ever before? What if, for instance, an AI model could accurately forecast a person's death?

Bose: Wait, what?!

Leffer: Yeah. It sounds really scary, right?

Bose: Uh, yeah.

Leffer: —and it might be, but probably not for the reasons you expect. I'm Lauren Leffer, tech reporting fellow at *Scientific American*.

Bose: I'm Tulika Bose, senior multimedia editor.

Leffer: And you're listening to *Scientific American*'s Science, Quickly podcast.

Leffer: So Tulika, death—we're all going to do it one day, but if you could know when you're going to die, would you want to?

Bose: Uh no, no, no no.

Leffer: You didn't even let me finish the question.

Bose: Yeah, I don't wanna know.

Leffer: Yeah, me either–seems like a super obvious case of TMI.

Bose: Yeah! For sure.

Leffer: But the inherently unsettling nature of "an AI calculator that spits out death predictions" didn't stop researchers from developing just that. The tool is called life2vec, and was described in a study published late last year.

Bose: And it's really an AI widget that says when you're gonna die?

Leffer: Yes and no. Life2vec isn't just a death predictor. It's way more general than that. It can offer more than just mortality forecasts. One big caveat right up front, though: It's hard to know exactly how accurate any of its predictions are at the moment–no one is claiming the tool can definitively predict an individual person's death. It's also trained on a very specific data set, namely one that contains information on residents of Denmark. So it can't offer meaningful predictions about anyone who isn't Danish.

Bose: OK, so that's a relief. But can we go back to the "more general" thing? What else can it predict?

Leffer: Yeah, so maybe it's a big deal for Danes. But on top of forecasting mortality over a four year period, the developers also tested their tool's ability to predict people's answers to personality questions and to forecast if someone would make an international move –

Bose: Interesting –

Leffer: – and to forecast if someone would make an international move. In all three of these tests, life2vec seemed to perform pretty well, with higher accuracy than other prediction methods the researchers compared it to. For the death test, that meant about 78 percent accurate, and moving abroad was about 73 percent.

Bose: Whoa.

Leffert: But again, it's hard to know exactly what accuracy means here.

Bose: Hold up, the death calculator could also predict personality traits and if people would live abroad? How? How are these things related?

Leffer: Let's take a step back. Life2vec is a machine-learning model, which basically just means it's a big computer program made to detect patterns in very large sets of data. The researchers built this model and trained it on tons of government-collected information on millions of people living in Denmark. They had employment history, basic demographic data, and also information on just about every interaction between people and the Danish medical system, because Denmark has universal health care.

Bose: Wow, that must be nice.

Leffer: Truly. Anyway, the researchers took all this data for each person and organized it into timelines. The life2vec model was fed all these timelines, and trained to pick up on patterns between the different events that show up in a person's life. So like, how are location and salary related? Do people diagnosed with certain diseases survive? Do people with certain professions tend to live longer?

Bose: Do people with certain career paths have certain personality traits?

Leffer: Exactly. That's how you can go from something like demographic info to personality questionnaire.

Bose: That's so interesting.

Leffer: From there, the researchers could ask versions of the model to make predictions based on all those timelines. The extra interesting thing with life2vec isn't just that it makes these predictions though–again, we've been doing that forever–it's how it does it. It's a type of model usually used for chatbots and language processing. It basically runs like souped-up autocomplete.

Bose: OK, wait, so the death predictions are like "autocompleting" someone's life?

Leffer: That is one way to put it. You give the model the life event timeline, you ask it a specific question, and it predicts the next relevant step in the timeline, based on the prompt. Sometimes that means predicting death.

Bose: Uh, kay yeah. This sounds way too much like a *Black Mirror* episode. Your phone's autocomplete starts to spit out "you'll die in seven days" type messages.

Leffer: Yeah, you should pitch that to Netflix.

Bose: I'm on it. We can be co-writers. So a little bit ago, you kept hedging on life2vec's accuracy, what was that about?

Leffer: Yeah, so I talked with some statistical and life modeling experts about this and none of them were super convinced by those 70+ percent accurate numbers that the researchers reported in the study. My favorite quote on this came from Christina Silcox, director for digital health at Duke Margolis Center for Health Policy. I asked her how powerful she thought life2vec's mortality predictions are and she said, quote, "I would not quit my job and go to the Bahamas based on this thing."

Bose: Haha, OK, that's kind of a burn.

Leffer: Yeah, it's more of a statement on how hard it is to predict something like death and to assess the accuracy of something so new–there's really nothing obvious to compare life2vec to.

Bose: So you can't just see how much better it is than flipping a coin or something.

Leffer: No. Data and statistics are wonky, particularly around death–which is a rare event, if you think about it. It only happens once in a person's life, and young people don't tend to die very often. In fact, if you were to just assume that everyone between like 25 and 50 in a population was going to live in a given year, you'd already be a really accurate death oracle. You'd be right most of the time.

Bose: Ah, OK, so that means you've gotta figure out what it means to actually be good at predicting death, and then compare life2vec to that, right?

Leffer: Totally! And that's the big question mark.

Bose: So what could you use this for, if not to tell you when it's time to go permanent vacation mode? If we don't know how good it is, what's the point?

Leffer: Great question. There are lots of potential uses–down the road, with more testing. For one, the model could help us understand disease prognosis and health outcomes. And from a sociology angle, which is where the study authors were really coming from, you can use life2vec to tease out hidden societal biases–links between age or country of origin and professional advancement.

Bose: All of that sounds theoretically cool, but I'm stuck on this idea, you know, that this will be used in a bad and scary way. Like, *Minority Report*-style punishing crimes before they happen, sort of stuff.

Leffer: It's a really valid concern!

Bose: Thank you for validating.

Leffer: Haha, of course. There is definitely an ethical risk with tools like this. The study authors were careful to note all the ways that Danish privacy and anti-discrimination laws restrict how life2vec can be used. It's not just going to be a freely available tool. Academic and government researchers will have to apply to use it for specified purposes, and they have a responsibility to protect people's data.

Bose: Ok, cool, that's better than nothing I guess.

Leffer: Yeah, and if it makes you feel any better–the study author I spoke with, Sune Lehmann, told me that he worked on this research because he trusts the Danish government, but in the U.S.–or another country without a comprehensive data privacy law–he probably wouldn't have been so comfortable.

Bose: You know, as someone living in the U.S., that doesn't make me feel better.

Leffer: OK, fair. Then to double down and make you feel worse: We kind of sort of already live in a version of the terrifying *Minority Report* world. In the U.S., there's predictive policing, and judges actually make sentencing decisions sometimes with the help of AI algorithms. In all of these cases, bias and innaccuracy are big documented problems that keep popping up.

Bose: Yeah, I mean, bias in AI is a huge issue. And I guess while we're talking algorithms, there's social media, too.

Leffer: Right, tech companies collect so much data on users and are certainly using that data to build predictive AI models that help companies maximize engagement or forecast what people will and won't buy. The biggest difference between the tech company algorithms, the criminal justice tools, and life2vec is that–for the first two–there's very little transparency. For the last one, the academic researchers want the public and the scientific community to understand how the tool works and what it can do.

Bose: All right, solid. To fight the system, I guess you have to understand the system.

Leffer: Yup, Lehmann's hope is that a transparent and flexible model like life2vec will spur conversation in a new direction–it might get people and governments to start thinking about what's possible and what's right. He told me, "I hope that this can be part of a discussion that helps move us in the direction of utopia and away from dystopia."

Bose: Utopia is a really big goal, but I hope he's right. Also I would settle for not dystopia. Honestly.

Leffer: Me too. Any zone in between that would be good with me.

Bose: I'm cool with that.

Leffer: It is a lofty goal. So Tulika, what have we learned here? I'm giving you a little test.

Bose: Uh, Denmark seems cool.

Leffer: A+, you passed.

Leffer: Science, Quickly is produced by Jeff DelViscio, Tulika Bose, Kelso Harper and Carin Leong. Our show is edited by Elah Feder and Alexa Lim. Our theme music was composed by Dominic Smith.

Bose: Don't forget to subscribe to Science, Quickly wherever you get your podcasts. For more in-depth science news and features, go to ScientificAmerican.com. And if you like the show, give us a rating or review!

Leffer: For *Scientific American*'s Science, Quickly, I'm Lauren Leffer.

Bose: I'm Tulika Bose. See you next time!

About the Author

Lauren Leffer is a contributing writer and former tech reporting fellow at Scientific American. *She covers many subjects, including artificial intelligence, climate and weird biology, because she's curious to a fault. Follow her on X @lauren_leffer and on Bluesky @laurenleffer.bsky.social.*

Elah Feder is a journalist, audio producer, and editor. Her work has appeared on Science Friday, Undiscovered, Science Diction, Planet Money, and various CBC shows.

Scientists Revive Human Retinas after Death

By Tanya Lewis

Few biological facts seem as irrevocable as brain death. It has long been assumed that when we die, our neurons die with us. But a new study on the neuron-packed tissue of the eye is beginning to challenge that dogma.

In the new work, researchers restored electrical activity in human retinas—the light-sensitive neural tissue that sits at the back of our eyes and communicates with our brains—from recently deceased organ donors. This achievement, reported in *Nature*, offers a better way to study eye diseases such as age-related macular degeneration, a leading cause of vision loss and blindness. It could also lay the groundwork for reviving other types of neural tissue and perhaps—one day—for retinal transplants.

Most retina studies are done in animals, primarily mice. But mouse retinas lack the macula, a key region found in human eyes that picks out fine details, so they are not an ideal model. Human eye tissue from autopsies often takes hours to obtain and is dead before scientists can study its function. But what if you could revive it?

When Yale University researchers showed in 2019 that rudimentary electrical activity could be restored in pig brains after death, University of Utah vision scientist Frans Vinberg, Scripps Research retinal surgeon Anne Hanneken and their colleagues were inspired to study whether retinal tissue could also be restored postmortem.

For the study, the researchers first tested how long mouse retinas could send electrical signals after the animals were euthanized. They were able to restore this activity up to three hours later—and found that a lack of oxygen was the main factor in irreversible loss of function. They then investigated human eyes that the researchers obtained from organ donors very soon after brain or cardiac death.

The scientists transported the eyes to the laboratory in a container that supplied oxygen and nutrients, then exposed the retinal tissue to dim light and measured electrical signals generated by the tissue. They were able to reestablish electrical activity in light-sensitive cells called photoreceptors, as well as in the neurons these cells connect to, in the donor eyes—if the eyes were obtained less than 20 minutes after death. Of course, the eyes could not "see," because they were not connected to a brain, Hanneken notes. But the results showed it was possible to restore not just individual retinal cells but the communication between them.

"What's most exciting is this really could become a model for studying visual physiology in human retinas, in health and in aging and in disease," says Joan Miller, chief of ophthalmology at Mass Eye and Ear and ophthalmology chair at Harvard Medical School, who was not involved with the new study. Macular degeneration, for example, has so far been difficult to study because living human eye tissue has been impossible to access. Using this new technique, scientists could study healthy and diseased donor eyes to understand their function and test treatments.

The team's findings also suggest it may be possible to revive other types of neural tissue. "The retina is a window to the brain, so if you can restore communication in the retina after death, it makes you pause and consider what kind of communication you might be able to recover in the brain," Hanneken says. The study additionally raises the prospect of retinal transplants, although those are likely still very far off, the researchers say.

This new work illustrates the importance of donor tissue to basic science. "We are very thankful for the donors and their families," Vinberg says. "We hope this will encourage people ... to check that box in their driver's license and also be willing to donate tissues for research."

About the Author

Tanya Lewis is a senior editor covering health and medicine at Scientific American. *She writes and edits stories for the website and print magazine on topics ranging from COVID to organ transplants. She also appears on* Scientific American's *podcast Science Quickly and writes* Scientific American's *weekly Health & Biology newsletter. She has held a number of positions over her seven years at* Scientific American, *including health editor, assistant news editor and associate editor at* Scientific American Mind. *Previously, she has written for outlets that include* Insider, Wired, Science News, *and others. She has a degree in biomedical engineering from Brown University and one in science communication from the University of California, Santa Cruz. Follow her on X @tanyalewis314 and Bluesky @tanyalewis.bsky.social.*

Humans Could Live up to 150 Years, New Research Suggests

By Emily Willingham

The chorus of the theme song for the movie *Fame*, performed by the late actress Irene Cara, includes the line "I'm gonna live forever." Cara was, of course, singing about the posthumous longevity that fame can confer. But a literal expression of this hubris resonates in some corners of the world—especially in the technology industry. In Silicon Valley, immortality is sometimes elevated to the status of a corporeal goal. Plenty of big names in big tech have sunk funding into ventures aiming to solve the problem of death as if it were just an upgrade to your smartphone's operating system.

Yet what if death simply cannot be hacked and longevity will always have a ceiling, no matter what we do? Researchers have taken on the question of how long we can live if, by some combination of serendipity and genetics, we do not die from cancer, heart disease, or getting hit by a bus. They report that with things that usually kill us omitted, our body's capacity to restore equilibrium to its myriad structural and metabolic systems after disruptions still fades with time. And even if we make it through life with few stressors, this incremental decline sets the maximum lifespan for humans at somewhere between 120 and 150 years. In the end, if the obvious hazards do not take our lives, this fundamental loss of resilience will do so, the researchers conclude in findings published in May 2021 in *Nature Communications*.

"They are asking the question of 'What's the longest life that could be lived by a human complex system if everything else went really well, and it's in a stressor-free environment?'" says Heather Whitson, director of the Duke University Center for the Study of Aging and Human Development, who was not involved in the paper.

The team's results point to an underlying "pace of aging" that sets the limits on lifespan, she says.

For the study, Timothy Pyrkov, then a researcher at a Singapore-based company called Gero, and his colleagues looked at this "pace of aging" in three large cohorts in the U.S., the U.K., and Russia. To evaluate deviations from stable health, they assessed changes in blood cell counts and the daily number of steps taken and analyzed them by age group.

For both blood cell and step counts, the pattern was the same: as age increased, some factor beyond disease drove a predictable and incremental decline in the body's ability to return blood cells or gait to a stable level after a disruption. When Pyrkov and his colleagues in Moscow and Buffalo, N.Y., used this predictable pace of decline to determine when resilience would disappear entirely, leading to death, they found a range of 120 to 150 years. (In 1997 Jeanne Calment, the oldest person on record to have ever lived, died in France at the age of 122.)

The researchers also found that with age, the body's response to insults could increasingly range far from a stable normal, requiring more time for recovery. Whitson says this result makes sense: A healthy young person can produce a rapid physiological response to adjust to fluctuations and restore a personal norm. But in an older person, she says, "everything is just a little bit dampened, a little slower to respond, and you can get overshoots," such as when an illness brings on big swings in blood pressure.

Measurements such as blood pressure and blood cell counts have a known healthy range, however, Whitson points out, whereas step counts are highly personal. The fact that Pyrkov and his colleagues chose a variable that is so different from blood counts and still discovered the same decline over time may suggest a real pace-of-aging factor in play across different domains.

Study co-author Peter Fedichev, who trained as a physicist and co-founded Gero, says that although most biologists would view blood cell counts and step counts as "pretty different," the fact that both sources "paint exactly the same future" suggests this pace-of-aging component is real.

The authors pointed to social factors that reflect the findings. "We observed a steep turn at about the age of 35 to 40 years that was quite surprising," Pyrkov says. For example, he notes, this period is often a time when an athlete's sports career ends, "an indication that something in physiology may really be changing at this age."

The desire to unlock the secrets of immortality has probably been around as long as humans' awareness of death. But a long lifespan is not the same as a long health span, says S. Jay Olshansky, a professor of epidemiology and biostatistics at the University of Illinois at Chicago, who was not involved in the work. "The focus shouldn't be on living longer but on living healthier longer," he says.

"Death is not the only thing that matters," Whitson says. "Other things, like quality of life, start mattering more and more as people experience the loss of them." The death modeled in this study, she says, "is the ultimate lingering death. And the question is: Can we extend life without also extending the proportion of time that people go through a frail state?"

The researchers' "final conclusion is interesting to see," Olshansky says. He characterizes it as "Hey, guess what? Treating diseases in the long run is not going to have the effect that you might want it to have. These fundamental biological processes of aging are going to continue."

The idea of slowing down the aging process has drawn attention, not just from Silicon Valley types who dream about uploading their memories to computers but also from a cadre of researchers who view such interventions as a means to "compress morbidity"–to diminish illness and infirmity at the end of life to extend health span. The question of whether this will have any impact on the fundamental upper limits identified in the *Nature Communications* paper remains highly speculative. But researchers have undertaken some studies–testing the diabetes drug metformin, for example–with the goal of attenuating hallmark indicators of aging.

In this same vein, Fedichev and his team are not discouraged by their estimates of maximum human lifespan. His view is that their research marks the beginning of a longer journey. "Measuring something is the first step before producing an intervention," Fedichev says. As he puts it, the next steps, now that the team has measured this independent pace of aging, will be to find ways to "intercept the loss of resilience."

About the Author

Emily Willingham is a science writer and author of the books Phallacy: Life Lessons from the Animal Penis *(Avery, Penguin Publishing Group, 2020) and* The Tailored Brain: From Ketamine, to Keto, to Companionship: A User's Guide to Feeling Better and Thinking Smarter *(Basic Books, 2021).*

How Old Can Humans Get?

By Bill Gifford

How long can human beings live? Although life expectancy has increased significantly over the past century, thanks largely to improved sanitation and medicine, research into hunter-gatherer populations suggests that individuals who escaped disease and violent deaths could live to about their seventh or eighth decade. This means our typical human lifespan may be static: around 70 years, with an extra decade or so for advanced medical care and cautious behavior. Some geneticists believe a hard limit of of around 115 years is essentially programmed into our genome by evolution.

Other scientists in the fast-moving field of aging research, or geroscience, think we can live much longer. A handful of compounds have been shown to lengthen the lifespans of laboratory animals slightly, yet some scientists are more ambitious—a lot more ambitious.

João Pedro de Magalhães, a professor of molecular biogerontology at the Institute of Inflammation and Ageing at the University of Birmingham in England, thinks humans could live for 1,000 years. He has scrutinized the genomes of very long-lived animals such as the bowhead whale (which can reach 200 years) and the naked mole rat. His surprising conclusion: if we eliminated aging at the cellular level, humans could live for a millennium—and potentially as long as 20,000 years.

How can that be? If aging is programmed, scientists could theoretically reprogram our cells by tweaking genes that are central to aging. This would require technology that we don't presently have, but Magalhães thinks it can be created. His great-grandfather died of pneumonia—a leading cause of mortality in the 1920s. When Magalhães contracted the same disease as a child, he was cured with a simple dose of penicillin. He thinks scientists can similarly develop therapies for aging, an endeavor to which he has now devoted his career. "I want to cheat death," he says bluntly.

[An edited transcript of the interview follows.]

Q: How has cheating death worked out so far?

A: I don't think we're going to have a drug that "cures" aging the way penicillin cures infections anytime soon. But a compound called rapamycin is quite promising. It extends lifespan by 10 to 15 percent in animals, and it is approved for human use, such as for organ transplant recipients. It does have side effects. I am optimistic that we will develop drugs akin to statins [taken daily to lessen risk of heart disease] that we take every day for longevity purposes. If you could slow down human aging 10 or even 5 percent, that would still be pretty amazing.

Q: How does rapamycin work?

A: Rapamycin does quite a number of things in the cell, but a lot of its effects [involve] slowing down growth and slowing down cell metabolism, which is why it has an impact on aging.

Q: Your grandmother lived to be 103 years old. Did she take rapamycin, or was her long life linked to something else?

A: I think it was the sun and the beach [*laughs*]. We know that to become a centenarian is mostly genetic. My grandmother didn't really exercise, and she didn't eat very healthily. She didn't smoke; she didn't have very bad habits, but she also didn't have particularly healthy habits. Yet she was quite healthy almost until the end–she was barely in hospital. With her it came down to genetics, environment, and some luck.

Q: You've sequenced genomes of very long-lived animals such as the bowhead whale, which lives up to 200 years. How are their genes different from ours, and what can we learn from them?

A: Various long-lived animals, such as humans, whales, and elephants, all have to cope with the same issues, such as cancer, but they use different molecular tricks to achieve their longevity. With bowhead whales, they seem to have much better DNA repair. My dream experiment is to take a bowhead whale gene and implant it in a mouse to see if the mouse would then live longer. Another obvious example would be the *p53* gene, which is very strongly associated with cancer suppression. Elephants have multiple copies of this gene, which makes them resistant to cancer. There are a few other candidate genes that we've discovered, not only in whales but in rodents such as the naked mole rat.

Q: Why are naked mole rats so interesting?

A: Naked mole rats are fascinating because they can live up to 30 years, yet they are smaller than a rat, which only lives to about four years. So you have a small rodent that's related to mice and rats but lives much longer and is very cancer-resistant.

Q: What's their secret?

A: In terms of cancer resistance and probably overall aging as well, it's their ability to respond to and repair DNA damage. But the threshold for a mouse cell to become a cancer cell is much lower than [the threshold] in humans. If you expose mouse cells to DNA damage, they will get cancer; if you expose naked mole rat cells to the same damage, it's going to be fixed. They won't get cancer.

Q: So if mice live several years, and naked mole rats live 30 years, and we live about 80 years, does that mean lifespans are genetically programmed?

A: The dominant theory of aging was about wear and tear–damage accumulating in our cells and components of our body like cars that break down over time. I've never really liked that because humans are not inanimate objects. There is damage, of course, and often aging seems to be very deterministic, almost like a program. A mouse will age 20 to 30 times faster than a human being. There are a lot of aging [characteristics] that just happen to everybody and even across species, such as loss of muscle mass. This doesn't seem like something that's random; it seems predetermined. So I think of aging as more akin to a software problem than a hardware problem.

My hypothesis is that we have a very complicated set of computerlike programs in our DNA that turn us into an adult human being. But maybe some of these same programs, as they continue into later life, become detrimental.

Q: What's an example of that?

A: A classic example would be thymus involution. Your thymus is a gland that produces T cells, which are very important to your immune system. But it disappears fairly early in life, around age 20—earlier if you're obese; later if you're an athlete. Basically it turns into fat. That strikes me as very programmatic. It's a classic case of antagonistic pleiotropy, where a process that is beneficial earlier in life becomes harmful later on.

Q: Why is the immune system important in aging?

A: The immune system, I think, is a low-hanging fruit in terms of targeting aging. It has systemic impacts, and it declines over time, which is why diseases like COVID become very dangerous to old people. But there are specific tissues, such as the thymus, that you can target for rejuvenation. To me, that's one way of starting. There are experiments in mice that show that if you change just one transcription factor [a protein that acts on genetic material], the thymus regenerates. In theory, I am convinced we can have radical interventions like this—to rewrite our genetic "software" and redesign human biology—to delay or even reverse aging. In practice, it is difficult, but in theory, I think there's a huge potential.

Q: How much potential is there? How long could we live if we got rid of aging?

A: I actually did some calculations years ago and found that if we could "cure" human aging, average human lifespan would be more than 1,000 years. Maximum lifespan, barring accidents and violent death, could be as long as 20,000 years. This may sound like a lot, but some species can already live hundreds of years—and in some cases thousands of years [such as the hexactinellid sponge and the Great Basin bristlecone pine]. If we could redesign our biology to eliminate cancer and evade the detrimental actions of our genetic software program, the health benefits would be mind-boggling.

Q: This sounds extreme. Are such profound interventions even possible?

A: I think it's possible. Is it going to happen soon? I think it's quite unlikely. Even if you can figure out how aging works, it is not easy to develop interventions. I am an aspiring science-fiction writer as well, and one thing I've noticed are these novels that are set 100 or 1,000 years from now, in a future with all kinds of technology that enables people to do incredible things, such as travel between stars—and people are still aging. But I think we'll figure out aging by then.

About the Author

Bill Gifford is co-author of the New York Times *bestseller* Outlive: The Science & Art of Longevity. *He ages in Salt Lake City, Utah.*

Would You Live Forever (If You Could)?

By Hillary Rosner

Recently, at a wedding reception, I polled some friends about immortality. Suppose you could upload your brain tomorrow and live forever as a human-machine hybrid, I asked an overeducated couple from San Francisco, parents of two young daughters. Would you do it? The husband, a 42-year-old M.D.-Ph.D., didn't hesitate before answering yes. His current research, he said, would likely bear fruit over the next several centuries, and he wanted to see what would come of it. "Plus, I want to see what the world is like 10,000 years from now." The wife, a 39-year-old with an art history doctorate, was also unequivocal. "No way," she said. "Death is part of life. I want to know what dying is like."

I wondered if his wife's decision might give the husband pause, but I diplomatically decided to drop it. Still, the whole thing was more than simply dinner-party fodder. If you believe the claims of some futurists, we'll sooner or later need to grapple with these types of questions because, according to them, we are heading toward a postbiological world in which death is passé–or at least very much under our control.

The most well-imagined version of this transcendent future is Ray Kurzweil's. In his 2005 best-selling book *The Singularity Is Near,* Kurzweil predicted that artificial intelligence would soon "encompass all human knowledge and proficiency." Nanoscale brain-scanning technology will ultimately enable "our gradual transfer of our intelligence, personality, and skills to the nonbiological portion of our intelligence." Meanwhile billions of nanobots inside our bodies will "destroy pathogens, correct DNA errors, eliminate toxins, and perform many other tasks to enhance our physical well-being. As a result, we will be able to live indefinitely without aging." These nanobots will create "virtual reality from within the nervous system." Increasingly, we will live in the virtual realm, which will be indistinguishable from that anemic universe we might call "real reality."

Based on progress in genetics, nanotechnology, and robotics and on the exponential rate of technological change, Kurzweil set the date for the singularity—when nonbiological intelligence so far exceeds all human intelligence that there is "a profound and disruptive transformation in human capability"—at 2045. Today a handful of singulatarians still hold to that date, and progress in an aspect of artificial intelligence known as deep learning has only encouraged them.

Most scientists, however, think that any manifestation of our cyborg destiny is much, much farther away. Sebastian Seung, a professor at the Princeton Neuroscience Institute, has argued that uploading the brain may never be possible. Brains are made up of 100 billion neurons, connected by synapses; the entirety of those connections make up the connectome, which some neuroscientists believe holds the key to our identities. Even by Kurzweilian standards of technological progress, that is a whole lot of connections to map and upload. And the connectome might be only the beginning: neurons can also interact with one another outside of synapses, and such "extrasynaptic interactions" could turn out to be essential to brain function. If so, as Seung argued in his 2012 book *Connectome: How the Brain's Wiring Makes Us Who We Are*, a brain upload might also have to include not just every connection, or every neuron, but every *atom*. The computational power required for that, he wrote, "is completely out of the question unless your remote descendants survive for galactic timescales."

Still, the very possibility of a cyborg future, however remote or implausible, raises concerns important enough that legitimate philosophers are debating it in earnest. Even if our technology fails to achieve the full Kurzweilian vision, augmentation of our minds and our bodies may take us part of the way there—raising questions about what makes us human.

I ask David Chalmers, a philosopher and co-director of the Center for Mind, Brain, and Consciousness at New York University who has written about the best way to upload your brain to preserve your self-identity, whether he expects he will have the opportunity to live forever. Chalmers, who is 50, says he doesn't think so—but that "absolutely these issues are going to become practical possibilities sometime in the next century or so."

Ronald Sandler, an environmental ethicist and chair of the department of philosophy and religion at Northeastern University, says talking about our cyborg future "puts a lot of issues in sharp relief. Thinking about the limit case can teach you about the near-term case."

And, of course, if there is even the remote possibility that those of us alive today might ultimately get to choose between death or immortality as a cyborg, maybe it's best to start mulling it over now. So putting aside the question of feasibility, it is worth pausing to consider more fundamental questions. Is it desirable? If my brain and my consciousness were uploaded into a cyborg, who would I be? Would I still love my family and friends? Would they still love me? Would I, ultimately, still be human?

One of the issues philosophers think about is how we treat one another. Would we still have the Golden Rule in a posthuman world? A few years ago Sandler co-authored a paper, "Transhumanism, Human Dignity, and Moral Status," arguing that "enhanced" humans would retain a moral obligation to regular humans. "Even if you become enhanced in some way, you still have to care about me," he tells me. Which seems hard to argue with–and harder still to believe would come to pass.

Other philosophers make a case for "moral enhancement"–using medical or biomedical means to give our principles an upgrade. If we're going to have massive intelligence and power at our disposal, we need to ensure Dr. Evil won't be at the controls. Our scientific knowledge "is beginning to enable us to directly affect the biological or physiological bases of human motivation, either through drugs, or through genetic selection or engineering, or by using external devices that affect the brain or the learning process," philosophers Julian Savulescu and Ingmar Persson wrote recently. "We could use these techniques to overcome the moral and psychological shortcomings that imperil the human species."

In an op-ed this past May in the *Washington Post* entitled "Soon We'll Use Science to Make People More Moral," James Hughes, a bioethicist and associate provost at the University of Massachusetts Boston, argued for moral enhancement, saying it needs to be voluntary rather than coercive. "With the aid of science, we will all be able to discover our own paths to technologically enabled happiness and virtue," wrote Hughes, who directs the Institute for Ethics and Emerging Technologies, a progressive transhumanist think tank. (For his part, Hughes, 55, a former Buddhist monk, tells me that he would like to stay alive long enough to achieve enlightenment.)

There is also the question of how we might treat the planet. Living forever, in whatever capacity, would change our relationship not just to one another but to the world around us. Would it make us more or less concerned about the environment? Would the natural world be better or worse for it?

The singularity, Sandler points out to me, describes an end state. To get there would involve a huge amount of technological change, and "nothing changes our relationship with nature more quickly and robustly than technology." If we are at the point where we can upload human consciousness and move seamlessly between virtual and non-virtual reality, we will already be engineering nearly everything else in significant ways. "By the time the singularity would occur, our relationship with nature would be radically transformed already," Sandler says.

Although we would like to believe otherwise, in our current mere mortal state we remain hugely dependent on—and vulnerable to—natural systems. But in this future world, those dependencies would change. If we didn't need to breathe through lungs, why would we care about air pollution? If we didn't need to grow food, we would become fundamentally disconnected from the land around us.

Similarly, in a world where the real was indistinguishable from the virtual, we might derive equal benefit from digitally created nature as from the great outdoors. Our relationship to real nature would be altered. It would no longer be sensory, physical. That shift could have profound impacts on our brains, perhaps even the silicon versions. Research shows that interacting with nature affects us deeply—for the better. A connection to nature, even at an unconscious level, may be a fundamental quality of being human.

If our dependence on nature falls away, and our physical ability to commune with nature diminishes, then "the basis for environmental concern will shift much more strongly to these responsibilities to nature for its own sake," Sandler says. Our capacity for solving environmental problems–engineering the climate, say–will be beyond what we can imagine today. But will we still feel that nature has intrinsic value? If so, ecosystems might fare better. If not, other species and the ecosystems they would still rely on might be in trouble.

Our relationship to the environment also depends on the question of timescales. From a geologic perspective, the extinction crisis we are witnessing today might not matter. But it does matter from the timeline of a current human life. How might vastly extended lifespans "change the perspective from which we ask questions and think about the nonhuman environment?" Sandler asks. "The timescales really matter to what reasonable answers are." Will we become more concerned about the environment because we will be around for so long? Or will we care less because we will take a broader, more geologic view?

"It's almost impossible to imagine what it will be like," Sandler says, "but we can know that the perspective will be very, very different."

Talk to experts about this stuff for long enough, and you fall down a rabbit hole; you find yourself having seemingly normal conversations about absurd things. "If there were something like an X-Men gene therapy, where they can shoot lasers out of their eyes or take over your mind," Hughes says to me at one point, then people who want those traits should have to complete special training and obtain a license.

"Are you using those examples to make a point, or are they actual things you believe are coming?" I ask.

"In terms of how much transhumanists talk about these things, most of us try not to freak out newbies too much," he replies obliquely. "But once you're past shock level 4, you can start talking about when we're all just nanobots."

When we're all just nanobots, what will we worry about? Angst, after all, is arguably one of our defining qualities as humans. Does immortality render angst obsolete? If I no longer had to stress about staying healthy, paying the bills, and how I'll support myself when I'm too old and frail to travel around writing articles, would I still be me? Or would I simply be a placid, overly contented ... robot? For that matter, what would I daydream about? Would I lose my ambition, such as it is? I mean, if I live forever, surely that Great American Novel can wait until next century, right?

Would I still be me? Chalmers believes this "is going to become an extremely pressing practical, not just philosophical, question."

On a gut level, it seems implausible that I would remain myself if my brain was uploaded—even if, as Chalmers has prescribed, I did it neuron by neuron, staying conscious throughout, becoming gradually 1 percent silicon, then 5, then 10 and onward to 100. It's the old saw about Theseus's ship—replaced board by board with newer, stronger wood. Is it or isn't it the same afterward? If it's not the same, at what point does the balance tip?

"A big problem," Hughes says, "is you live long enough and you'll go through so many changes that there's no longer any meaning to you having lived longer. Am I really the same person I was when I was five? If I live for another 5,000 years, am I really the same as I am now? In the future, we will be able to share our memories, so there will be an erosion of the importance of personal identity and continuity." That sounds like kind of a drag.

Despite the singularity's utopian rhetoric, it carries a tinge of fatalism: this is the only route available to us; merge with machines or fade away—or worse. What if I don't want to become a cyborg? Kurzweil might say that it's only my currently flawed and limited biological brain that prevents me from seeing the true allure and potential of this future. And that the choices available to me—any type of body, any experience in virtual reality, limitless possibilities for creative expression, the chance to colonize space—will make my current biological existence seem almost comically trivial. And anyway, what's more fatalistic than certain death?

Nevertheless, I really like being human. I like knowing that I'm fundamentally made of the same stuff as all the other life on Earth. I'm even sort of attached to my human frailty. I like being warm and cuddly and not hard and indestructible like some action-film super-robot. I like the warm blood that runs through my veins, and I'm not sure I really want it replaced by nanobots.

Some ethicists argue that human happiness relies on the fact that our lives are fleeting, that we are vulnerable, interdependent creatures. How, in a human-machine future, would we find value and meaning in life?

"To me, the essence of being human is not our limitations ... it's our ability to reach beyond our limitations," Kurzweil writes. It's an appealing point of view. Death has always fundamentally been one of those limitations, so perhaps reaching beyond death makes us deeply human?

But once we transcend it, I'm not convinced our humanity remains. Death itself doesn't define us, of course—all living things die—but our awareness and understanding of death, and our quest to make meaning of life in the interim, are surely part of the human spirit.

Referenced

Citizen Cyborg: Why Democratic Societies Must Respond to the Redesigned Human of the Future. James Hughes. Basic Books, 2004.

The Singularity Is Near: When Humans Transcend Biology. Ray Kurzweil. Viking, 2005.

Brain Cuttings: Fifteen Journeys through the Mind. E-book. Carl Zimmer. Scott & Nix, 2010.

Connectome: How the Brain's Wiring Makes Us Who We Are. Sebastian Seung. Houghton Mifflin Harcourt, 2012.

About the Author

Hillary Rosner is a freelance writer based in Colorado. She has written for National Geographic, *the* New York Times *and* Wired, *among other publications.*

GLOSSARY

atherosclerosis The buildup of substances such as cholesterol and fats in the walls of arteries, blocking blood flow.

autolysis The self-destruction of cells by their own enzymes.

biogerontology The study of the biological processes of aging.

cardiopulmonary resuscitation (CPR) An emergency procedure involving chest compressions intended to help save someone's life when their heart has stopped or they have stopped breathing.

centenarian A person who is 100 or more years old.

corporeal Having or relating to a physical body.

decomposition The process by which organic substances rot or break down into simpler types of matter.

lucidity Clearness of expression or thought.

metabolic Relating to processes that a living body uses to handle a particular substance.

mortality Death or the state of being something subject to death.

mortality salience The awareness of the inevitability of death and the anxiety that causes.

numinous Possessing a strong spiritual or religious quality, arousing spiritual or religious emotion.

postmortem Occurring after death.

resilience The ability to recover from or adapt to challenges.

rigor mortis The stage at which muscles stiffen after death, resulting in a stiffening of the limbs.

sepsis A life-threatening condition when the body's immune system has an extreme response to injury or infection.

FURTHER INFORMATION

Blasdel, Alex. "The New Science of Death: 'There's Something Happening in the Brain that Makes No Sense'," the *Guardian,* April 2, 2024. https://www.theguardian.com/society/2024/apr/02/new-science-of-death-brain-activity-consciousness-near-death-experience.

Catanese, Lisa. "Longevity: Lifestyle Strategies for Living a Long, Healthy Life," Harvard Health Publishing, June 25, 2024. https://www.health.harvard.edu/staying-healthy/longevity-lifestyle-strategies-for-living-a-healthy-long-life.

Illing, Sean. "The Science of Near-Death Experiences," *Vox*, May 25, 2024. https://www.vox.com/the-gray-area/351128/the-science-of-near-death-experiences.

Miller, Lisa. "Beyond Death: The Science of the Afterlife," *TIME,* April 20, 2014. https://time.com/68381/life-beyond-death-the-science-of-the-afterlife-2/.

Morrow, Angela. "End-of-Life Stages Timeline," Verywell Health, May 2, 2024. https://www.verywellhealth.com/the-journey-towards-death-1132504.

Raymond, Chris. "What Happens When You Die?," Verywell Health, August 19, 2024. https://www.verywellhealth.com/what-happens-to-my-body-right-after-i-die-1132498.

Reardon, Sara. "Burst of Brain Activity During Dying Could Explain Life Passing Before Your Eyes," *Science*, May 1, 2023. https://www.science.org/content/article/burst-brain-activity-during-dying-could-explain-life-passing-your-eyes.

Samuel, Lawrence R. "The Psychology of Death," Psychology Today, March 8, 2019. https://www.psychologytoday.com/us/blog/psychology-yesterday/201903/the-psychology-of-death.

Stein, Rob. "Debate Simmers Over When Doctors Should Declare Brain Death," NPR, February 11, 2024. https://www.npr.org/sections/health-shots/2024/02/11/1228330149/brain-death-definition.

CITATIONS

1.1 Dust to Dust: The Brief, Eventful Afterlife of a Human Corpse by Arpad A. Vass (September 1, 2010); 1.2 "Necrobiome" Reveals a Corpse's Time of Death by Christopher Intagliata (December 22, 2016); 1.3 Why Humans Live So Long by Heather Pringle (April 1, 2015); 1.4 Aging Is Linked to More Activity in Short Genes Than in Long Genes by Diana Kwon (January 6, 2023); 1.5 Live Long and Proper: Genetic Factors Associated with Increased Longevity Identified by Nicholette Zeliadt (July 1, 2010); 2.1 What Near-Death Experiences Reveal about the Brain by Christof Koch (June 1, 2020); 2.2 Lifting the Veil on Near-Death Experiences by Rachel Nuwer (May 14, 2024); 2.3 Some Patients Who 'Died' but Survived Report Lucid 'Near-Death Experiences,' a New Study Shows by Rachel Nuwer (September 14, 2023); 2.4 Why Dying People Often Experience a Burst of Lucidity by Jordan Kinard (June 12, 2023); 2.5 Thinking about Death Can Make Life Better by Michael W. Wiederman (April 1, 2015); 2.6 The Legal Definition of Death Needs to Be Clearer by Ariane Lewis (February 14, 2024); 3.1 There Is Nothing Normal about One Million People Dead from COVID by Steven W. Thrasher (February 10, 2022); 3.2 Death by Primordial Black Hole by Avi Loeb (June 6, 2021); 3.3 The U.S. Just Lost 26 Years' Worth of Progress on Life Expectancy by Tanya Lewis (October 17, 2022); 4.1 A Common Antibiotic Could Prevent Deaths from Childbirth Complications by Allison Parshall (February 9, 2023); 4.2 ECPR Could Prevent Many More Cardiac Arrest Deaths by Erica Westly (November 27, 2023); 4.3 Ways to Extend Your Healthy Years, Not Just Your Life by Lydia Denworth (November 1, 2023); 4.4 Eat (Less) to Live (Longer) by Nikhil Swaminathan (September 20, 2007); 4.5 Why the Life Expectancy Gap between Men and Women Is Growing by Lori Youmshajekian (November 14, 2023); 5.1 Is Death Reversible? by Christof Koch (October 1, 2019); 5.2 Never Say Die: Why We Can't Imagine Death by Jesse Bering (October 1, 2008); 5.3 Why the "You" in an Afterlife Wouldn't Really Be You by Michael Shermer (July 1, 2017); 5.4 Can AI Predict Your Death? by Lauren Leffer, Elah Feder, and Tulika Bose (January 22, 2024); 5.5 Scientists Revive Human Retinas after Death by Tanya Lewis (August 1, 2022); 5.6 Humans Could Live up to 150 Years, New Research Suggests by Emily Willingham (May 25, 2021); 5.7 How Old Can Humans Get? by Bill Gifford (July 31, 2023); 5.8 Would You Live Forever (If You Could)? by Hillary Rosner (September 1, 2016)

Each author biography was accurate at the time the article was originally published.

INDEX

M

N

O

P

Q

R

S

T